Beep You!
You BeepHole

The Black Book of Indian Cuss & Slurs

Beep You! You BeepHole

The Black Book of Indian Cuss & Slurs

Smarak Swain

Srishti
PUBLISHERS & DISTRIBUTORS

SRISHTI PUBLISHERS & DISTRIBUTORS
N-16, C. R. Park
New Delhi 110 019
srishtipublishers@gmail.com

First published by Srishti Publishers & Distributors in 2011

2nd impression

Typeset in AGaramond 11pt. by Suresh Kumar Sharma at Srishti

Printed and bound in India

THIS is a work of FICTION

NOTHING in this fiction – narrated in first person or otherwise – is written with considerations of factual accuracy.

The fiction is written in the form of lecture handouts by a fictitious researcher to an academic audience. Every chapter is a separate lecture.

Contents

Vol 1

1
Teri Maa Ki

Colours and Contours of Gaali

I missed saying “bhenchod” to people who understood it. It does not mean “sister fucker.” That is too literal, too crude. It is, rather, punctuation, or emphasis, as innocuous a word as “shit” or “damn.” The different countries of India can be identified by the way each pronounces this word – from the Punjabi “bhaanchod” to the thin Bambaiyya “pinchud” to the Gujarati “bhenchow” to the Bhopali elaboration “bhen ka lowda.” Parsis use it all the time, grandmothers, five-year-olds, casually and without any discernable purpose except as filler: “Here, bhenchod, get me a glass of water.” “Arre, bhenchod, I went to the bhenchod bank today.”

Suketu Mehta *(Maximum City)*

I’ve tried to reduce profanity but I reduced so much profanity when writing the book that I’m afraid not much could come out

—Ernest Hemingway

Some wise man had once said that to learn a new language, there are four major steps: first, learn how to greet girls in that language. Second, learn its swearwords. Third, learn commonly used words, and lastly learn the grammar. This wise man may not be absolutely correct (may be because the wise man I refer to is me: this is my theory) but makes a strong point: the importance of curses to a language. Language survives culture by being a common means of communication between people of that culture. While languages are as varied as cultures are, there are some similarities between various languages. One of these is the nature of curses.

In most languages you find swearwords... and there are similarities of semantics cutting across language barriers. For instance, the fact that the mother-son relationship is special in all mankind, a common swearword in all languages is mother-fucker, or what they call *maderchod* in Hindi, *ma-gian* in oriya and *aii-zhavedaa* in Marathi. Yet, the display of cuss in public, or in literature, varies from culture to culture. The usage of maderchod in Hindi is as widespread as fuck is in English. Yet, the mention in Hindi literature, and films, of swearwords is very low. This may be because ours is a hypocritical society. For instance, we talk of karma and dharma, while at the same time engaging in institutionalised inhuman behaviour towards untouchables.

My first brush with swearwords

I was in class seven then... or maybe six. I learnt the word "*magian*". Anything that is a taboo always arouses curiosity and excitement in children's circle. No wonder, magian had the same effect. At first, we knew not the literal meaning of the term. Then slowly the meaning became clear, as the dawn of adolescence drove away the ignorance of innocence. Then I learnt other Oriya cusses, and later Hindi ones. It was fashionable to swear at a friend, just to show that you dare defy the taboos of society.

Both in secondary and high school, I have marked that Hindi and Oriya swearwords suffered from an inferior status to English swearwords. Those who prefer to swear in English seem to believe that they are more polished and refined, and that vernacular swearwords are the stuff used by street children and the illiterate. It is unfortunate that while Dick and *Lowda* mean the same thing, one is fashionable while the other is looked down upon. Perhaps the colonial hangover of English favouritism hasn't even left curses: curses, which should have the same egalitarian status cutting across barriers of caste, creed, race etc. Another point of view on this issue is that may be Dick and Lowda do not really compare on levels of harshness. A gaali spoken in one's own native tongue is always more severe than one spoken in a second language. Even if this is the case, vernacular swearwords are usually branded as 'gutter tongue'.

IIT Days

An individual from middle class background best understands the real essence of *gaalis* – swearwords – in an engineering college. You get to know that there is more to a curse than the semantic meaning. The word *maderchod*, for example, assumes several meaning depending on the feelings with which it is expressed. If someone cracks a seven-figure-a-year package in campus placement, you say "*phod diya be maderchod, phod diya*"[¥]

If someone cracks a PJ, or spreads some funny gossip, you fondly say

[¥] You have cracked it maderchod, you have cracked it!

"*Hat maderchod*, shut your *chut* mouth up"[¥€]

If someone is shagging behind closed doors and you want to spoil his bliss, you bang on the door and say

"*Nikal maderchod*. Abe that porn star looks like your sister"[ъ]

If you want a favour from someone, you affectionately say

"*Mera* homework *kar de na maderchod*... I will treat you a maggi at Cheddies"[Ψ]

And pat will come the reply " *Mujhe chutia samajh rakha hai kya... itna chuda hua code and just a maggi? Nothing less than a mader dinner in LS will do*"[ʢ] Here mader is used to mean four-course. Gaalis are an expression of feelings – both positive and negative. Ironically, in engineering colleges swearwords only imply positive emotions. If you want to insult a chap and you blurt out the word maderchod, the whole dialogue gets diluted. Hence, never use gaali when you want to really hurt the person concerned. Use *shudh* pure language.

Besides maderchod, there are two other common gaali specializing on the incest: *behenchod* and *betichod*. This is where Hindi diverges from English. In English you don't find swearwords like sister-fucker or daughter-fucker in common usage. But behenchod and betichod are quite cool gaalis. For instance, if there is a chutia around who thinks it is really bad to use the gaali maderchod, you can use the word betichod for him (just see to it that he doesn't have a kid). These are usually the people who have been over-socialized into values

[¥€] Stop it maderchod, shut your cunt mouth up

[ъ] Get out maderchod... that port star looks like your sister

[Ψ] Please do my homework maderchod... I will treat you a maggi at Cheddies restaurant

[ʢ] Do you take me for a chutiya? Just a maggi for such a fucked up code! Nothing less than a mader dinner in LS will do

and morals by their parents; they would even feel guilty if you say they fuck their wives, and strongly deny the accusations.

Now, do you know when to use the word behenchod? I mean, I have often seen people use the word maderchod at places where behenchod is more suitable and behenchod at places where maderchod sounds better. The advantage of behenchod over maderchod is that you can screw the syntaxes to produce varied sounds. For example, there is behenchod, and there are versions like vhanchod, bhaaaanchod, and benchod. Due to this, the effect of behenchod is more than that of maderchod when you intend to have a dramatic stretch.

Colours of Gaali

Psychologist **Carl Jung** had once said that there is a collective unconscious that pervades throughout mankind. This collective unconscious is a psychic entity that an individual inherits from his/ her previous generation. Most gaalis, I believe, are archetypes of this collective unconscious. In every language you will find swearwords concerning mothers (she got knocked and bore a baby before marriage/ she is a slut/ whore/ she has incest relations etc), and genitals. Yet, it is incorrect to state that Dick and *Lund* mean the same thing, or Dick and Dong for that matter. It is not just the literal meaning but also the *feelings attached* that finally make a word. *Lund*, *chut*, *gaand*, and their derivatives have multiple usages in Hindi grammar.

Lowda means someone who is a Dickhead, *Landura* means an Idiot. *Ling*, on the other hand, is used in reference to Lord Shiva and His hugeness that even porn stars are jealous of. *Maa-Ka-Lowda* again has a reference to mothers.

Chutia is perhaps the most used cuss in usage in Hindi belt of India. It really is a harmless word, meaning idiot, or fool, or stupid depending on the context in which it is used. Still it is a taboo for the simple reason that etymologically it means someone who has come out of a *chut*. I wonder who hasn't. The word *chut* is itself so severely sexist that it is seldom used, though in IIT Kharagpur swearing chut had become a fad by the time I reached final year.

"Abe *chut*, why haven't you met your project guide. He is really pissed and is ready with a *khada hua lund* for you" (*khada hua lund* means erect penis).

"*Chutad*, you don't even know how to hack into a porn site".

"That's a *chutiatic* computer you have. It is even slower that a P2 processor".

And then there were other derivates like *chut-ke-dhakkan*, *chut-ke-baal* (also called *jhant*), pink chut, *kaali chut*, *chutiapa* etc. Those days I used to force my friends to read my short stories. Those who got frustrated with my stories used to say "Abe *chutiapa* mat kar, ask someone else to read it. I read only Champak and Mastram"

Another word, *bhonsadi*, again means cunt. This word is quite popular in UP and Bihar (and areas where migrants from these states have settled) but not used quite often elsewhere. *Bhonsdi wale* means one who has come out of a cunt. Surprisingly, in most engineering colleges wherein UP bhaiyajis and Biharis have a dominance this word is used as a title to address the dearest of friends.

At this point, I must explain the conceptual difference between *chut* and *bhonsadi*. Even I wasn't conceptually clear on this, so I referred to few friends from Hindi heartland. According to them, a *burr* is a virgin cunt, while a *bhonsadi* is one in post-delivery period. A chut is a cunt which isn't virgin but hasn't yet delivered. I know this sounds sick, but as a scholar my job is to maintain value-neutrality in presenting facts. Also the usages of the two terms *bhonsadi wale* and *chutia* are vastly different.

Swearword	Literal meaning
Burr	Genitals of a virgin female
Chut	Genitals of a female who has lost her virginity but has never delivered a baby.
Bhonsadi	Genitals of a female who has delivered a baby.

Table 1.1 Various swearwords based on female genitals

"This new prof in vlsi lab is a big *chutia*. He has no clue what's happening in experiments"

"B*honsadi wale*, he is a little strict so you think he is chutia. Trust me, he is quite sharp"

Gaand has become such a colloquial word that it no longer borders in the area of taboo words. Yet, the censor board is wary of letting moviemakers use it in movies: shows the kind of hypocrisy existing in our society. A band from XLRI even uses this word in one of its compositions nicked GMD: "*Tere gaand mein danda re...*".

Creativity and Gaali

If you have watched the Irish movie "*lock, stock and two smoking barrels*", you know how the flavour of gaalis can be harnessed to make creative prose, poetry, and motion pictures. My personal favourite in the movie is by Barry the Baptist: "No mortgages, no debts; lock, stock, the fuckin' lot".

Unfortunately, this is an area which hasn't yet been explored to that extent in vernacular language media. Luckily, you get many chances to hone your gaali-creativity skills during ragging in engineering colleges. For example, during ragging session in a wing in my hall in Kharagpur, I was asked to give an innovative gaali to another wing. I shouted at the top of my voice to the fellows in the other wing,

"Teri maa ko antenna pe dalke chodunga
Tera baap tv mein dekhke muth marega"

(I will fuck your mom on an antenna
And your father will masturbate over it when he sees it on TV)

At this point I would like to present a poem. This poem was collectively written by Graduate Trainees (GTs) of Tata Steel of 2006 batch and dedicated to a so-called *landura* GT, named Arian Mukherjee (name changed):

The Poem	Rough English Translation
Arinita meri raand	Arinita my *Raand* (whore)
Aaj dikhaegi na apna gaand	I hope today I will get your *gaand* (arse)
Tu hai meri kaamdhenu	You are my holy cow
Main hi tera saand	I am your *saand* (Bull)
Kulta kulakchani kalmuhi	Kulta kulakchani kalmuhi
Kuch zyada hi chaudi hai teri gaand	Somewhat too wide is your gaand
Tere liye to hai bas ek hi funda	For you there is just one funda
Tere gaand mein hota rahe danda	Your gaand be perpetually fornicated with a *danda* (stick)
Agar ek ke liye ho tu bhari	If you are too much for one
To sab ghusao baari baari	Then pals lets all enter one by one.

No wonder, when the poem was circulated via SMS in the whole batch, this guy was in tears. After this, he stopped being the dickhead that he was.

Gaali as a way of life

There are some people for whom gaalis are a way of life. They can't do without swearing in every sentence. Take, for example, my friend Meepak Dallik (name changed). He used to start his day with the chant of *Banda* (Oriya for Dick) and kept using the work in every sentence till his mouth shut with sleep at the end of the day.

"Banda whose class we have today?"

"Banda I am hungry"

"Banda I need to pee"

"Banda I like that maal"

"Banda you are a good friend of mine" etc

He also used to make use of innovative curses like *ghoda-gian* (horse fucker), *pimpudi-gian* (ant fucker), *benga-gian* (frog fucker) etc. Unfortunately, he is married now and has reformed quite a lot. The world of swear-lovers has lost a great patron.

By the way, if you want to meet some great patrons of swearwords, meet some Jats from Delhi. In their characteristics accent, they make use of many colourful swearwords. A Jat property broker in Delhi who had fixed me a room for my UPSC preparations used to use some sort of gaali in almost every sentence. He often referred to his youngest son as a *maderchod* because the fellow was useless and did not work!

"...see! His elder brothers have all got some good jobs. I ask this *maderchod* to at least help me in my business, but he doesn't care"

2
Introduction

Conceptualising gaalis vis-à-vis swearwords, slurs, and slang

When a gentleman is disposed to swear, it is not for any standers-by to curtail his oaths

—William Shakespeare

All philosophies, if you ride them home, are nonsense, but some are greater nonsense than others.

—Samuel Butler

Kosi, the sorrow of Bihar, cuts right through Mithilanchal region of the state. The river is young, undulating and there are numerous rapids. The river also marks the natural boundary of Maithili tongue and Theth tongue. People to the east speak Maithili and people to the west speak Theth. Maithili is a sweet language. Theth, on the other hand, is supposedly crude and foul. Theth is a mixture of Hindustani and Maithili, yet considered bad language. 'Theth' literally means crooked/ twisted, and people in other regions of Mithilanchal resist from speaking this language.

I wonder how a whole language can be considered bad language! On a higher level of analysis, can language be good or bad? The essential feature of language is that it's arbitrary. 'Fuck', 'father', 'shit' and 'scooter' are all arbitrary words and do not mean anything. However, these words act as symbols in English language and hence convey meaning. Being symbols words convey a variety of objects and subjects. Words convey emotions, double meanings, hidden meanings, conscious and unconscious urges and motives, and punctuations too.

Gaalis are an essential part of language in the sense that they *convey* strong emotions. Every language has its own set of gaalis. Some languages (such as Theth) have more, others less[1] . All that gaalis convey is also not always cognizable to the common man. When a common man tells *chutiya* he may simply imply idiot, but there are numerous other symbols that the gaali may carry. First its literal meaning: one who has come out of a *chut*. Then there is the inappropriateness of using a word derivative of female genitals, which is symbolic. Chutiya is highlighted when used in normal conversation, which is symbolic of emphasis added to the meaning. This work is basically an attempt at making sense of these symbols.

Gaali and Swearing

A first step in conceptualisation of gaali is differentiating it from swearing. In spirit, gaalis play similar role as swearwords in language. Yet gaali is different from swearwords. My contention is that gaali is not an *exact* translation of swearing in Hindi. To understand this difference, we need to understand what constitutes swearing.

One of the most objective definitions of swearing has been provided by Andersson and Trudgill. According to them, swearing is a type of language use in which the expression:

- Refers to something that is taboo and/or stigmatised in culture
- Should not be interpreted literally
- Can be used to express strong emotions and attitudes.[2]

An expression or word that fulfils all the three conditions above can be termed swearing. Taboo is a critical condition for a word to be branded as swearword (alternatively called cuss-word). Many scholars use taboo words and swearwords interchangeably, although not all taboo words are swearwords.

Dear Readers,

have you heard that joke: whoever says yes is a maderchod; whoever says no is a behenchod?

A taboo is 'an inhibition or ban resulting from social custom or emotional aversion'[3]. Being socially prohibited, taboos concern such arenas of social interaction such as religion, supernatural beliefs, disease, body organs, and sex. For example, it is a taboo in Hindu communities to eat beef. Sexuality is the 'most tabooed aspect of human existence'[4] and talking about sex in public is a taboo in most societies.

There are two types of taboo: behavioural taboo and verbal taboo. Swearwords derive from verbal taboo. The word 'fuck' is a verbal taboo because it refers to having sex. Interestingly, while 'fuck', 'sex', and 'intercourse' all are verbal taboo, only 'fuck' is a swearword. That too the word has to be used in a non-technical sense in order to qualify as swearing. If you say 'I have had lots of beauty and boobs. Fucking does not excite me anymore' or that 'I do not like porn movies which have only fucking without any story' you use the word in a technical sense, to imply the act of having sex. Fuck is a taboo because it *means* sex, but if it is *used to* mean sex (i.e. in a technical sense) it is not swearing.

Lastly, swearwords can be used to express strong emotions and attitudes, but more of that in a later chapter.

Gaali (cf. गाली) is different from swearwords in the sense that a word need not be taboo word in order to qualify as gaali. Gaali literally means 'to abuse'. A word does not have to be tabooed or stigmatised in society in order to qualify for being a gaali. A word or expression seeking to disparage or humiliate a subject or a group of subjects also qualifies as gaali. Hence, expressions and words of the nature of ethnic slur are also gaali. This is because slurs

Gaali & lingo

KLPD stands for *Khade Lund pe Dhokha*, i.e. disappointment to an erect penis. This abbreviation is a lingo used by college students to refer to anything which does not come up to one's expectation. KLPD is used in its most literal sense when you find a girl extremely hot at a glance or from rear but later find her cold and so so.

The 'L' in KLPD stands for lund which is a gaali. Hence some people confuse it for swearword. However, KLPD is used as a synonym for disappointment and is not insulting. Hence this is technically not a swearword. Another less frequently used word BCD – *Bheege Chut pe Dhokha* – is however a gaali because it is considered sexist and insulting.

are heavily loaded with prejudices and stereotypes about an ethno-social group (may be a racial, religious, language or caste group). Based on this conclusion, I conceptualise gaalis as a multiplicity of groups of words which fall under the following heads:

1. Taboo
   a. Genital
   b. Anatomical
   c. Incest
   d. Vulgarity & obscenity
   e. Scatological
   f. Prostitutes and Eunuchs
   g. Handicap
2. Slur
   a. Sexist
   b. Ethnic – racist, casteist, religious.
3. Animal names

1. Taboo

There are two primary sources of taboo in Indian societies: body parts and sex. Sex is perhaps the most suppressed issue of public talking. Sex is vulgar and talk about sex is often considered obscene. As a result, Hindi words *chod* and *thok* both implying sex are gaalis. Anal sex, oral sex, and masturbation also become verbal taboos by extension.

Genitals, hidden that they remain behind layers of clothing, are body organs used for sex. Other anatomical features such as arse and breasts are also considered taboo. Incest is a behavioural taboo in *every* human society. Gaalis alluding to incestuous relations are a projection of this behavioural taboo. Scatological taboos refer to verbal taboos regarding excrement and other bodily wastes. *Shit* and *crap* are swearwords that refer to scatological functions.

Sex being such a tabooed aspect of our society, prostitution and sexual deviance are stigmatised. A 'whore' is a human being who is a taboo in decent society, hence has to live on the margins. Taking the name of red light districts is considered improper, so what if these places are the most pleasant hangout for many. Whore and son-of-a-whore are common swearwords in most languages, derived from this stigmatisation of prostitution.

Yet another group who live on the margins of society are transsexuals and eunuchs, those who are termed *hijda* in our society. Hijdas have a strong symbolic presence in Hindu belief system; a hijda's blessing is considered auspicious while her curse is feared. Still no one identifies with a hijda. A man assessed as not man enough or who behaves like a girl (in situational mannerisms) is often abused as hijda or *hijde.*

While sex workers and transsexuals are socially deviant, handicapped individuals are physically handicapped. Handicap is a situation that attracts both pity and disgust from people. People do not openly ridicule a person of physical handicap; yet his handicap is ridiculed in private. When you seek to hurt or humiliate this person or a relative of his, you utter the ridicule on his face. In the Mahabharata story, when Duryodhan mistakes an illusion (in Indraprasta's royal palace) for a water body, Draupati comments that he is blind just like his father. It is said that this gaali was the root cause behind Kurukshetra War – a war Duryodhan fought to satiate his hurt ego.

As compared to physical handicap, mental handicap is more openly ridiculed. There are many individuals who may not be socially as smart as you, or are absentminded, or may be truly idiots. If you find tough to tolerate them you disparage such an individual as *chutiya, gaandu*, *bewakoof*, or *ullu* all implying idiot or fool. These terms are taboo when used against a person who is truly a retard.

2. Slurs

Slurs are a class of gaali that are disparaging in content (if not intent), and can be used to express strong emotions and attitudes. The attitudes expressed are usually negative (i.e. prejudicial) and are loaded with false beliefs. The intent of the slur-giver may or may not be to humiliate or hurt the receiver; still the receiver or any other person may find it quite offensive. For example, people from West Maharashtra find the word *ghati* insulting. I may call an individual (say Gita) from the region ghati just out of fun, without any ill-intention. Gita may or may not find it insulting. Even if Gita does not find it insulting, any other person from the region may take exception to my calling Gita ghati. This is because slurs are often symbolic of false beliefs and negative attitudes towards a group as a whole.

Broadly two types of slurs are discussed in this work. Sexist slurs are remarks and comments that demean female gender and/or seek to stereotype them. Ethnic and xenophobic slurs are negative gaalis against ethnic communities (mostly minority communities) that put them in bad light.

3. Animal names

Man, I am sure at some point in your life a lady friend has called you a dog or a pig. That's because her feelings invariably get hurt, no matter what. Logically if you have hurt her feelings she should not call you by an animal name. Animals are not capable of hatred or envy; they have far simple personalities than you, hence not really capable of hurting your lady friend's feelings. Perhaps her intention was to cope with her sentiments by abusing you with a certain class of gaalis: animal names.

Which animal names would constitute gaalis? Of course a receiver won't mind being called a lion (*sher* in Hindi) or tiger. That would be a complement. It is the animals with low status in our mental perception that become victims of gaali vocabulary: dog, pig, owl, rat, donkey, and insects to name a few. Which animals have a low status actually depends on their lifestyle and our mythologies. Those animals which are considered sacred by the standards of mythology are not usually given a low status. Most of our Gods and Goddesses have their own exclusive carriages driven by specific animals: Shiva rides a bull, Kali rides the tiger, and Vishnu flies across on a big eagle. Animals like dog and pig do not have significant visibility in mythologies.

Dogs have a low status because they eat anything you throw at them, and follow you everywhere with a wagging tail. Street dogs additionally hover around stingy places in search of leftovers. Pigs hover underground, in the gutters, in search of food. Both dogs and pigs practice coprophagia: the act of eating faeces. Hence the swearword swine.

Ullu ka pattha is a common mild gaali in Indian neighbourhoods. It may very well be one of the first gaalis children learn as they grow up. The gaali literally means 'offspring of an owl' but is intended to mean 'offspring of a fool'. What's intriguing about the gaali is that ullu (owl) is an auspicious bird in Hindu belief. Lakshmi, the Goddess of fortune and wealth, rides an owl as she moves through the homes of lucky few who get rich. Hence owl is a symbol of prosperity, not foolishness in the least. However, *ullu ka pattha* is an Urdu gaali and derives its root from Persian. In Persian society, owls have a low status. Hence the meaning fool for *ullu.*

Gaali	Literal Meaning	Implied meaning
Kutta/ kutte	Dog	Various meanings; used frequently and meaning depends on the context
Soowar	Pig	Various meanings
Soowar ka aulaad	Offspring of a pig	Various meanings
Gadha	Donkey	Stupid
Ullu	Owl	Fool
Ullu ka pattha	Son of an owl	Son of a fool, fool
Gandde naali ka keeda	Insect of a filthy gutter	Someone of lowly birth or background
Geedad	Jackel	Coward, gutless

Table 2.1 Hindi gaalis based on animal names

Note that the word 'bitch' is not a swearword belonging to this class. It is a taboo word. In their mating season, female dogs have lot of sexual heat. Plus they let male dogs ride them ('doggy style') anywhere in public. Hence the word was originally used for women as an insult meaning one of low morals or one hungry for sex (similar to slut in usage). Subsequently the word became so common in usage that now it has myriad meanings.

Swearwords are an integral part of any language, and Indian vernaculars are no exception. Unfortunately writings on swearwords and slurs in Indian literary space are few and dispersed. Hence many people are not aware of the real import of gaalis and what emotions they convey; what functions they play in human and social health. Nor has significant attempt been made to understand etymological origins of gaalis. Besides, there are many related issues of contemporary relevance such as censorship, racist comments and ethnic slurs. This book is an attempt at an organised study of street literature and parochial linguistics.

This chapter makes an attempt at conceptualising 'gaali' viz-a-viz swearwords and slurs. The word gaali is used rather than swearwords in this book because although quite overlapping gaali is an indigenous concept.

Chapter III, IV, and V discuss gaalis that are directed at specific groups of people. Chapter III discusses expletives used to make derogatory reference to members of female gender. Chapter IV makes a brief survey of popularly used ethnic slurs and chapter V is a continuation of ethnic slurs with specific reference to xenophobia. Chapter VI, VII and VIII take a critical look at sociology of gaalis while Chapter IX discusses the utility of gaalis.

Chapter X examines issues of law and censorship. Chapter XI (in volume 2) is actually a self-help guide to cuss control for those having a problem of uttering gaalis at the wrong place. Chapter XII is a basic guide to cussing culture across India.

There are a few points I would like the reader to take stock of. First, I have made liberal use of cuss words in this book. One could not possibly write about cuss words without using them. Secondly, even though this is a study of gaalis I have abstained from using academic language or academic structures of writing. This being a book on bad language I have taken the liberty of using my own language and expression. We Indians are multilingual peoples who think in native tongue, talk in Hindi, and read in English. Hence to discuss swearwords I found Hinglish the most comfortable alternative to write in. This book is written in Hinglish.

INSET # 2.1 TABOO WORDS IN ENGLISH AND HINDI AT A GLANCE

Taboo	English		Hindi	
	Taboo but not vulgar	***Vulgar***	***Taboo but not vulgar***	***Vulgar***
Sex	Intercourse Coitus Copulation	Fuck Screw Bang Fornication	यौन-क्रिया [Yaun-kriya] संभोग [Sambhog]	Chod (n) Chodna (v) Thok (n) Thokna (v)
	Anal sex	Bugger	Guda-maithun	Gaand marana Gaandu
	Oral sex	Suck	Mukh-maithun	Mooh marna (v) Choos le
Genital & Anatomical	Penis	Dick Dickhead Cock Prick	Ling	Lowda Lund
	Vagina Vulva	Cunt Pussy	योनि [yoni]	Chut Burr Bhonsadi
	Breasts	Boobs Tits	Stan	Chuchi
	Buttocks	Arse/Ass	Guda	Gaand

Masturbation	Oranism	Wanker Tosser	हस्तमैथुन [Hasta-maithun]	Hilana (v) Muth marna (v) Sadka marna (v)
Incest		Motherfucker	–	Maderchod
		Sister fucker		Behenchod
Scatological	Feces	Shit Crap	Pakhana Hagna	–
Socially deviant groups	Sex workers	Whore Tart Hooker	Yaun karmi	Randi Chinaar Gastee
	Transsexual & cross-dressers	Eunuch	Hijda	Hijda Hijde Chakka
Physically/mentally deviant groups	Mental Handicap	Idiot Moron Retard	Murkh	Chutiya Gaandu Ullu

3

Of Maals and Items

Sexist gaalis at a glance

A woman reading Playboy feels a little like a Jew reading a Nazi manual.

—Gloria Steinem

Thence lady readers are requested to take extra discretion before delving into contents of this chapter

From an analysis of generic gaalis of indigenous India we now move on to gaalis that are more specific and coarse in content and intent. While the gaalis discussed in *Teri Maa Ki* are, for the most part, harmless the gaalis that will be discussed in this essay are discriminatory and prejudicial in nature and demonstrate a latent complex of superiority among men.

There are multiple manifestations of this complex in Hindi language, but none as trivial as the word *maal.* Maal roughly means a babe, or what they call in English as an 'item'. Maal is used to refer to a girl who looks exceedingly hot. Did you say hot? Well, that would mean a compliment to any girl. How can maal be termed profane in Indian colloquial dialect? The word is no doubt slang as it is not considered standard in Hindi dialect or language. There is also a high degree of vulgarity associated with the usage of the word. But can it be considered a profanity? Well, I found this a debatable issue in conceptualization of gaalis.

For better understanding of this issue, I did a small experiment. I wrote an entertaining blog post explaining the concept of maal. In this blog post, I had intentionally assumed a sexist tone and had made numerous sexist comments making use of the word maal. Even though I had put up a disclaimer explaining that the purpose of the post was creative writing, I got very strong reactions from readers of the fairer sex. While a few ladies in fact enjoyed the blog, most of them were quite negative towards the way I dealt with the subject. For the benefit of the reader, I hereby reproduce part of the blog post and few of the comments by female readers:

"...*maal* literally means goods. A stationary shopkeeper, for example, means notebooks and pens when he says that maal has to be delivered to him. This implication attaches a bitter taste to the word. This is because women like to believe that they are human beings; that they have brains, and personality, and that they are not just objects of desire (perhaps this is why some people rightly believe that women in general are delusional). Another reason may be that maal as a word is used mostly by the loafers in any college. The so-called sophisticated girls take offence when labelled so.

A Taxonomy of Maals

In engineering colleges, an elaborate taxonomy is followed by students to brand girls. Girls of engineering colleges, indeed, have a hard time. They are branded the way clothes, or for that matter shoes are. And the branding is done singularly on the basis of looks and assets. The logic is that (engineering college students base all their arguments on logic) girls are but objects of desire.

Broadly speaking, there are three types of girls in IIT Kharagpur:

1. Maals
2. Males and
3. Non-males

Maal, male, and non-male subsumes many different varieties of girls. Maals are those who are sexy, beautiful, and have assets in terms of, to put it crudely, butts and boobs. Non-males may be:

1. Beautiful but not endowed with assets, for example the *manchesters* who have chests like men
2. Endowed with assets but not beautiful (for this category of girls, the best customer base is that of those who can *cover the face and fuck the base*)

Males, on the other hand, are those who are just like one of us. If you are damn despo, you go for these girls.

Now, within the category of maals, there are many sub-categories. The simplest label is that of *tanak maal*. It simply means a really high quality maal. In every batch in IIT Kharagpur, you will find one, and only one, tanak maal. She usually is well-proportioned, has boastable vital stats, and looks good. If the batch is lucky, she may b extra-curvaceous. And then there are the girls of other colleges who visit kharagpur for spring fest, or tech fest, or some conference. Some of these may be just better than the in-house tanak maal, and hence labelled as *bakchod maal*. If a group of friends see such a maal somewhere in the campus, everyone stares at her as if she is some sort of alien. One of them would quip:

"*Bakchod maal hai be... koi try maro na yaar*"

(She is a Bakchod maal. Someone try on her)

Another may even say "*nahi yaar, patakchod maal hai*"

(No man, she is better than a Bakchod maal... in fact she is a Patakchod maal)

Patak-chod maal is the next higher quality of brand. It means one who is irresistible – you just have a look at her and u want to patak her (as in crash her on the bed, or sofa, or garden, or road, or the most comfortable place available in the vicinity) and get into the act. It shows the kind of self-restraint, or strength of character that we possess.

Now, you must realize the fact that these brands are but relative and very subjective. A girl who is a *tanak maal* for someone may be a *bakchod maal* for another, and *patakchod maal* for still another. As an IITian, for example, I have a very low threshold to classify some girl as patakchod maal. The first time when I reached Delhi for UPSC preparation, my friend Vikrant had asked me to meet him in CP. At CP, waiting for him, I couldn't help glaring at every girl who passed me. Practically every girl was a *patakchod* maal. I couldn't believe that there could be any place on earth full of patakchod maals. Slowly, I got accustomed to the fact that Delhi is one of the most fashion-conscious places and girls here like to look sexy. Every girl in Delhi University North Campus was a model. I used to go to DU central library just to stare at these divas. Why the library? Bcoz u would look like a psycho, or worse a stalker, if u do so on the road.

But this is where another problem in classification comes. If all are patakchod maals, how do you typify them? So my friend Amit, an expert in this field, came up with some more classificatory criteria. For example, there can be *in-built maals* or *parlour maals.* In-built are those who are born maals. Whereas parlour maals are those who buy beauty in parlours. Later, however, my friend CMT who is a hapshot corporate honcho (he sells premium cosmetic products like lipsticks, face creams etc for HLL) refuted that the concept of in-built maal is a myth. This is an ugly world, and HLL makes it beautiful. Given the fact that he is but a salesman for HLL, we should take his words with a pinch of salt. The point is beauty isn't a virtue. In the ultimate Marxian analysis it is an ideology used by the daughters and wives of the bourgeoisie to assert their fake superiority to daughters and wives of the proletariat.

The next level of classification is that some are *spankable maals.* Here we are graduating from *sadakchap*[5] Hindi to Hinglish. Spankable maals are those whose best part is the butt. You feel like spanking same. This label is most popularly given to Punjaban gals. Some pals complain they have had a hard time controlling their bloody hands from reaching out to a stranger's butts. I don't know how they manage to do it, but many girls wearing tight jeans walk such that the butts look like two huge, tasty cakes that move up and down alternately.

Yet others are labelled *doodwali maals* -meaning maals who are reservoir of milk. Never ever, even by mistake, mention this to a girl, however cool and dude-type she seems. Bcoz this kind of label shows only how sick and pervert some men are. Basically it refers to those girls who have huge headlights. But then there is a catch here. Though silicon enhancement of breasts isn't yet popular in India, most girls look bigger than their size. This may be the result of usage of push-up bra. One girl I used to regularly eye in DU library (technically I wasn't a stalker... I never meant no harm) sometimes looked much bigger and much smaller other times. At first I was really puzzled by how it was possible. It took me quite some time to solve the puzzle: push-ups. Hence, think twice and ascertain by periodic observation, if possible, before labelling any maal as doodwali.

And then there are the BHMB maals: *Badi-hoke-maal-banegi.* I know what you are thinking now: can't this bastard leave children? See, dear reader, my job here is just to make a value-neutral analysis. Well, in Delhi even school girls are pretty look conscious. You start strolling in Old Rajinder Nagar around six in the evening and you will find yourself ogling at school kids. These kids have an advantage in dressing: since they aren't old enough they have the social sanction to wear more provocative dress (and parents don't realize the kind of perverts who stay in the vicinity). At the same time, they seem to mature much earlier than many small-town girls. By maturity I mean physical maturity -these girls seem to have outgrown their age under the effect of some kind of steroid. Some of my friends who used to enjoy ogling at these school girls even feared that they might have crossed over to pedophile-dom.

While BHMBs are at one end, MLAs are at the other end of the spectrum of maals. MLAs – maal like aunties – are the ladies who have crossed over to motherhood but have been careful enough to *maintain* themselves. Most of us men have, at one point of time or other, fancied older women. Let alone fancy MLA, most guys of our type are even open to marriage with an older woman. Hence, the popularity of MLA in teen friends' circle. If at all you are interested in MLA fantasy of young men, watch the movie Malena – perhaps the best portrayal of youth fantasy for older women.

Before ending the discussion on taxonomy of maals, I would like to make a small reference to geographical variations in maals. I am not much of a judge of how different maals are across length and breadth of the country. This puts me at a disadvantage, and I request the reader to further explore the authenticity of what follows. It seems like Delhi maals are shallow; they are more materialistic and prefer a biker over a blueline-bus-commuter. On the other hand, Bombay maals are more philosophical. Talk some rubbish, abstract stuff and you can trap one. It also seems that Bombay maals are less pretentious, and more natural than Delhi maals. While Delhi maals pretend to be sophisticated, Bombay maals really are. To trap a Delhiite maal, you don't have to be pretentious: just be ready to make a hole in your purse and she is yours. On the other hand, to get along with a Bombaykar maal you have to pretend that you are broad-minded, that you respect her as a person and an equal, and worse make her believe that she isn't just an object of desire for you, but a human being!"

The taxonomy in this blog post was actually narrated to me by a friend and I had just put it in words. But I was the one who had to deal with the volley of angry feedback that came about from my lady readers. Most of them did not leave a public comment and preferred to talk to me in person. One of the public comments I got – posted as anonymous – was:

> Mr [—]… after reading your post, I couldn't stop my fingers 4m typing this… I agree post mod[ern] writings can be on

> anything and everything under the sun or 4 that matter even beyond the sun... but ur post reflects pure perversion n nothing else.... I was just wondering... maybe even I have been mentally raped by guys like u... n ds iz leaving me with a strange kind of discomfort coz I would never know that a so called decent looking person sitting with a book in his hands is actually analysing my breast size n what not... anyway what is leaving me more tense is... if I have daughter in future, how would I save her 4m getting mentally raped even before she is an adult...

Against this criticism, I also received comments defending the content and intent of my article. All of these being from male readers can be discounted. What is it that offends women about the word *maal*? And more importantly for this work of research, can *maal* be termed profane?

Women as objects

To make sense of this puzzle, we now look into some ideas prevalent in gender psychology. Objectification is an attitude or belief that regards a person as a commodity[6]. This kind of attitude not only undermines the personality of the 'object' but also deeply impacts the self-esteem of the victim. When you look at the person as an object of sexual pleasure, the attitude you manifest is called *sexual objectification*.

The word maal literally means 'goods' and is most frequently used by traders in purchase and sale of goods. In another sense it may mean 'good quality goods'. It is this meaning which is implied when a woman is branded as maal, and as has been made clear from the typology presented above 'good quality' is exclusively judged on the basis of looks and assets. Hence maal is a manifestation of sexual objectification in Hindi language.

In fact, maal gaalis are the most harmful of all gaalis. This is because maal gaalis are directed towards an entire gender of human society, and seek to degrade the gender. Whenever you call a hot girl 'tanak maal', even if the girl does not hear it you reinforce a belief about female inferiority. In a way, maal gaalis are a form of subtle sexism. Subtle sexism refers to sexist jokes that tend to denigrate women. The general belief is that such remarks and jokes are harmless, but research has shown that women are negatively affected by subtle sexism[7].

The psychological impact of such gaalis can be two ways: (1) for some women such gaalis lead to demoralisation and decreased self-esteem. A lady friend of mine once observed that she feels beauty is a curse. Because she is beautiful, men make a value judgment about her the moment they see her. Because she is beautiful she does not know if a guy who is so good to her is a friend or has some ulterior motive. She had got exceedingly good marks in the interview round of civil service exams conducted by UPSC, which got her into IAS. Because she was beautiful, her achievement was undermined and many fellow candidates stated that the interview board gave her good marks because she is a 'patakchod maal'. Interestingly, even not being physically beautiful is also a problem. You get lewd comments from losers, such as *Cover the face and fuck the base.*

Another totally different impact of maal gaalis (and sexism in general) on the psyche of women is (2) the formation of *objectified body consciousness.* Basically when people around a woman show attitude of sexual objectification, she tends to believe that she has to be a desirable sex object in order to be accepted by people. Some of these women internalise the attitude of sexual objectification and aspire to become sex objects. This has become a very prevalent psychological phenomenon among the youth population of our generation. You must have observed that these days many Bollywood songs contain the word 'baby' and 'maal'. One of the songs starts like this:

"Heyy Babyy
jee lene de is pal ko,
kal ki sochenge kal ko..."

Neither the mood nor the meaning that the lyricist wants to present in this song is evident from the usage of 'baby'. Yet another song starts like this:

"Karle baby dance wance,
Dance wance dance wance,
Give me soniye chance wance,
Chance wance chance wance..."

There is also a genre of music videos, perhaps the most popular in recent times, performed by 'item girls' and 'baby dolls'. Frankly, most of my favourite numbers belong to this genre, and I don't complain. I am mad about baby doll Sophia and wish I had that doll in my room to play with (the *Kanta Laga* baby will also do). The point to note is that the general objectification of women has seeped into collective unconscious of Indian mass and projects itself in popular entertainment.

If maal be at one end of sexist gaalis, **males** and **non-males** are at the other extreme. Gaalis belonging to this group are in the nature of slurs, disparaging women for the lack of 'perceived beauty'. Every woman is a work of art and every woman is beautiful in her own way. Yet not all of us humans perceive beauty the same way. Hence you may find some women beautiful, some unattractive. Problems arise when you make value judgment on a woman *you* find unattractive. Indians generally have an infatuation for fair skin; hence a lady with milky fairness is called *makkhan* (literally butter, means a girl whose skin you feel like licking). On the other hand, many tend to look down upon a *kaali laundia* (literally 'black girl'). Yet others evaluate women on the basis of assets. The ideal woman (typified by screen models) should have big, fulsome breasts. One who is not a manchester or carromboard.

Such slurs are most frequently used against women one finds smart and better than himself. When a man finds a woman better than himself, it hurts his male ego and he tries hard to demean the girl so as to boost his self-esteem. If he finds the girl unattractive, he naturally slurs at her looks. This male ego is a dangerous thing. The other day, a lady colleague of mine was felicitated for presenting a new revenue collection model. Many guys who have been working on similar projects and have not found success obviously did not like it. When she went up the stage and delivered a smart lecture, a colleague muttered:

Na chut na chuchi
Mein sabse achi

(Neither cunt [looks] nor breasts,
But I am the best)

A variant of this comment is:

Na chut na chuchi
Nakhre Noor Jahan ke ('NC NC NN JK')

(Neither figure nor breasts,
But attitude that of a beauty queen)

Above phrase is a popular slur used in office places against confident and intelligent women not conforming to the beauty stereotype. When using this slur, one may recite the whole phrase or have a laugh by citing the phrase in codes such as 'na-chu-na-chi' or 'NC-NC-NN-JK'.

The conclusions we can derive from above analysis are:

- o Gaalis are words or phrases that are insulting, rude, vulgar, or show disrespect.
- o The maal group of words and phrases are vulgar and rude.
- o Maal words show disrespect at least to the woman intended at.
- ➢ Hence 'maal' and its derivatives are gaalis. Words such as 'males', 'non-males', and carrom-board/ manchester which demean women whose physique does not conform to the expectation of certain men are also gaalis.

Now whether it is right or wrong to use maal gaalis? Dude, it is all up to you. My job here is just presentation of facts and analyses (nor am I under the perception that you would follow what I say). But yes, if a girl is comfortable with being called 'item' and 'baby', you sure can call her maal. If she takes offence, she does so because of her conception of inferiority of slang Hindi (what many call *sadapchap* language). A primary purpose of this work is to create awareness for a social movement to give indigenous cuss words their due.

INSET 3.1 COMMON SEXIST GULLY GAALIS IN INDIA

SEXIST GAALIS			
Maals		*Males, Non-males*	
Erotic symbolism	Body part objectification	Beauty based slurs	Body parts based slurs
Tanak maal patakchod maal Chamiya	Doodwali maal Spankable maal Makkhan	Kaali chut Bhaddi	Manchester Lemon/ Nimbu Carromboard NC-NC-NN-JK

Note:

- *Kaali chut* literally means black pussy and is used derogatively against people of dark skin colour.
- *Bhaddi* literally means ugly.
- *Nimbu* (lemon) and carromboard have meanings synonymous with Manchester.

Makkhan literally means butter and is used to imply both fair complexion and a body as tempting in taste as butter.

4

Brown Indians, Chinky Indians

The prevalence of ethnic slurs

Racism is an ism to which everyone in the world today is exposed; for or against, we must take sides. And the history of the future will differ according to the decision which we make.

—Ruth Benedict

JK Rowling had introduced a swearword in the Harry Potter series as early as the second book. It being primarily a children's story, she could not have possibly introduced an expletive referring to sex or body organs. The word she introduced was mudblood, a derogatory word for muggle-born wizards. Since none of her readers was a muggle-born wizard no one actually took offence, yet mudblood is to Potter's world what *nigger* is to an African-American in America: a cuss.

Ethnic and racial slurs are a category of swearwords quite similar to other categories, yet much different from them. For one, these slurs are *always* directed towards an ethnic community. If someone tells me 'you look like a *chamrau*' it is an insult to people from Chamar caste community rather than me. What is implicit in you-look-like-a-chamrau is a prejudice – a sweeping negative generalization about all members of a community.

Prejudices towards the out-group being a natural tendency, peoples tend to stereotype each other, most often negatively. Gaalis disparaging a particular group or community are not only an expression of this stereotyping but also a tool for further discrimination against the community. For example, if a self-respecting university student is called *chamrau* because he is from the Chamar caste the gaali does more damage than evident. It (1) points towards the traditionally low status the caste has had in society, (2) implies that the student has forgot his *auqaat* (status) and worse (3) states that he would be better off tanning leather[8] than studying.

Indian society has always been a multi-ethnic one. Yet our society is not a melting pot but an uneasy co-existence of various ethnic groups. Creating boundaries is one of the prime preoccupations of Indians. To differentiate 'civilized society' from the aborigines, we created the *Jana-Jati* divide[9] . *Jana* refers to the aborigines while *Jati* refers to society of caste Hindus. Within the civilized *Jati* society numerous *jatis* (castes) were created to institutionalise discrimination. And then there are the Muslims who are different from Hindus; the Dravidians who are darker than Aryans; and Orients who are… uhh… Nepali. In such a society prejudices are bound to run high. Higher prejudices mean more racism, more stereotyping, more gaalis.

Racism in India

Given our long history of racial discrimination by colonial rulers, it may sound absurd at first that Indians would indulge in racism. After all everyone but Indians and dogs were allowed entry into select White clubs in India. At least, to be sure there is no racial bias against people of colour. We ourselves are 'brown', although this word is kind of misleading. Indians come in various sizes and colours. Within a single family one may find people of various shades.

However, even if discriminatory feelings are low, prejudices are there. For example, all people from South India are termed *madrassis.* During British rule whole of South India was included in the Madras province, hence the word. Madrassi is a derogatory term but not always used as a gaali as such. In the 1990s, the nativistic movement of Shiv Sena was directed against South Indian immigrants in Bombay. At that time *madrassi* was used as a disparaging gaali, the way *bihari* is used today to disparage North Indian immigrants. Shiv Sena had in fact come out with numerous other gaalis for South Indians, such as *yandugundu wala* and *lungi wala.* People hailing from the Western Ghat region of Maharashtra take deep offence if referred to as *ghati* in other parts of the state.

It is tough to say if *bihari* is a formal word or slang or swear. Anyone from Bihar is a Bihari, and even if you swear *bihari* at a Bihari with prejudicial and rude overtures I doubt he would mind. Yet there is a stigma added to the word Bihari. Two years back, when I was in Delhi preparing for civil services I had tried to get a flat for three friends in Rajinder Nagar. All three were from Bihar. Using my contacts I had set up their meeting with few landlords – all of them Punjabi (most real estate in the area being owned by people of Punjabi origin). While these estate owners were initially cordial and welcoming, their attitude changed the moment my friends revealed that they are Biharis. Later a senior had revealed that most of the civil service aspirants holed up in Rajinder Nagar are Biharis but many lie to their landlords: that they are from Kolkata or Kanpur. This is because of the prejudices many Delhiite Punjabis have about Biharis: that they are untrustworthy trouble creators. There is also a widespread belief that most thefts are a handiwork of immigrant Biharis.

Later my friends did get a good flat, having claimed that they are Bengalis. Much later the Punjabi landlord had introduced one of them to a Bengali gentleman staying in another floor, and his bluff got busted. The landlord had then wryly commented 'These Biharis... they lie all the time. You can never trust them.'

These days in formal conversation use of Bihari as a word is discouraged. 'People of Bihar' is a reasonable alternative.

Gaalis like *madrassi* and *bihari* are pretty localized, and are not used extensively by general public. A more severe and diffuse ethnic slur is *chinky*. This slur is widely used in certain Western countries (such as US and UK) so also in India against Mongoloids and other people with oriental features. In India, the word is mostly used to refer to our compatriots from North-East.

The use of chinky is so widespread in places like Delhi and Bangalore (these cities have high population of students from North-East) that most people using the word don't realise that the word is racist. I myself used to use the word without any idea of what it means. I also had a perception that chinky is derived from the word China. But no, the word is derived from the English word chink which means a small opening. Chinky is used as a simile for small or slanted eyes that is characteristic of oriental look.

Another ethnic slur with reference to people from North East is *bahadur*. Bahadur is a term referring to the guard who patrols your residential neighbourhood in the night. Incidentally many of these guards, till the 1970s and 80s, were Nepali. Hence *bahadur* became a derogatory word to refer to Nepalis. The nescience among general populace is so high that they don't differentiate between Nepalis and Indian citizens from North East. Many of my friends from North-East have complained that in mainland India most people consider them Nepali. Most illiterate people are just not aware of the existence of Nagas, Monpas, and Mizos as our people. It also does not help that the visibility of North-East in Indian movies and politics is so low. Hence, mainland people confuse North-East Indians with Nepalis. As a result bahadur has become a racial slur on people from North-East too.

Gulute (pronounced gultee) is a slang word for Telugu people. G-U-L-U-T-E is actually a rearrangement of letters in T-E-L-U-G-U. In Kharagpur campus, we Oriyas were referred to as *uddu*. I was often fondly called an *uddu bandar* (Oriya monkey) by my friends. Tamils are often referred to as *tami* (sounds like Tommy which is a name given to dogs). Bengalis are referred to as *bongs*. But these are mostly harmless slang words, rarely meant as swearword. So why are chinky and bahadur taken so offensively?

One reason, a friend who hails from Manipur tells me, is that such words pit North-Easterns as 'them' versus 'us' (mainland people). It makes them feel like aliens (or second class citizens) in their own country, which in turn creates an identity crisis in their psyche.

Another reason is that words like *gulute*, *tami*, and *uddu* don't point towards any ethnic prejudice; they are 'lingos' used in slang dialects. But *madrassi* when used by people from other parts of India when referring to South Indians points towards a feeling of superiority;

South Indians are seen as an inferior race when this word is used. Similarly swearwords 'chinky' and 'bahadur' point towards stereotypes and prejudices. Chinkys are dog-eaters, their food is stale and smells. They are flat-faced and short-tempered. Chinky girls are easy going and would give you sex with ease if you woo them. These are some of the false beliefs associated with using the slur chinky.

Yes, dog-meat is eaten in Nagaland. But there is no reason to generalise this over all of North-East; nor is it right to attach a negative connotation to this. Cultures vary in their traditions, and there are many other cultures where dog meat is relished. North East dishes such as Jado, Galpo and Smoked Pork with Axone are food items I relish. They produce a strong aroma, but are extremely healthy and hygienic food. Even in Orissa and Bengal people relish *sukta macha* (dried fish) which produces strong aroma when cooked. The belief that orient looking people are short-tempered perhaps comes from a fear of the stranger. Interaction between brown Indians and orient Indians is low even when they stay in the same locality. Hence they remain strangers. Another reason is the association of martial arts (and Bruce Lee, Jet Li et al) with oriental looking people. A stranger who can give flying kicks and tiger-claw punch is obviously dangerous.

Girls from North-East are the trendiest of all Indians. Traditionally they don't wear sari or salwar, and in contemporary times they prefer western wear. It is their lifestyle, their culture. Also gender parity being high in North-East these girls are confident and more bold than girls from the mainland. All these put together create an image in mainland men that they are of a loose character. This is strictly a case of ethnocentrism.

Interestingly people from mainland are also subject to racism in

North-East! It is all relative, you know. In Mizoram, for example, people from the plains are called *vais*. This word is used in contempt to refer to the long-nosed people who look 'different' from Mizos[10]. Etymologically *vai* is derived from the Hindi word *bhai* which means brother. When people-from-the-plains first interacted with Mizos, they called Mizos *bhai* as a friendly gesture. Mizos reciprocated this gesture by calling the guests *bhai*. However, Mizos could not pronounce *bhai* (the letter 'bha' being absent in their language)and so pronounced the word as *vai*. In due course *vais* became a word to refer to people-from-the-plains. With the large immigration of people from mainland India, insecurity and fear grew among Mizos. This insecurity pitted 'them' (*vais*) against 'us' (Mizos) and *vais* became a ethnic slur[11].

Similarly, the word for people from the plains in Manipur is *mayang*. *Mayang*, in Meitei, means foreigner. Many incidents of racial attacks and abuse on outsiders have been reported in Manipur[12]. While the word *mayang* can be used in a non derogatory sense, it becomes derogatory in usage when sentiments of hatred are attached. That racial discrimination is prevalent in Manipur is a surprising trend; perhaps there is no other state of India which boasts of the kind of racial fusion that is existent in Manipur. The yellow-skinned Meiteis (of Kuki-Chin racial stock) and the dark-skinned Bishnupriya Manipuris (Aryan racial stock) had entered Manipur during different periods from East and West respectively. But over the centuries these two races have constructively interacted in cultural and social life. Today Manipur society is a composite of people with Dravidian, Aryan, Pong, Siamese, and Chinese racial origin.

The SCientiST in IIT

There is significant conceptual ambiguity one faces in analysing ethnic slurs pertaining to religion and caste. For example, the word *kafir*[13] means a non-believer in Islamic doctrine. But in contemporary times this word is used by Muslims to refer to non-Muslims, who do not obviously believe in Islamic religion. Now if a Muslim uses *kafir* to make a derogatory remark on a Christian, can this be called a gaali? The Christian does not take it as an insult for he is indifferent to Islamic religious beliefs. Yet the Muslim gentleman has delivered a disparaging, ethnocentric comment.

DIKU

Tribal population of Jharkhand call all people from the plains 'Diku' which means foreigner. The slur came into popular use during the Santhal rebellion (1855-1856) and Munda rebellion of Birsa Munda; Diku was then used as a term to incite tribals to resist foreigners which included Indian landlords and British colonialists. Diku was also used in ideological debates during Jharkhand movement for statehood. After the formation of Jharkhand the word has almost lost its slur character. The overtone of hatred and prejudice is but subliminal.

Similarly, if a member of Bhangi community is called *bhangi* it is no doubt discriminatory but the problem is discrimination is built into the caste system. So can *bhangi* be called a gaali? The real import of a word actually depends on the context in which it is spoken and the emotions involved in cussing. Due to these ambiguities, I seek not to dwell into this topic in detail. Rather I find it more fruitful to look into more contemporary forms of casteist gaali.

Back in my days in IIT Kharagpur, I had attended a lecture by an alumnus in which he talked about European universities as a study option for Indian students. The alumnus said that the university is a place where people from diverse background come together. And it is not difficult to find a few losers who would subject you to racial ridicule. I can't say about European universities, but such was the case in Kharagpur at least.

It was only in my third year in Kharagpur that I heard the word *scientist*. Or I might have heard the word before but did not understand its meaning; the word sure is deceiving. Every professor and every researcher in Kharagpur is technically a scientist. But not every one of them is a ***scientist***. *Scientist* is a derogatory word referring to students who have availed of SC/ST reservations[14] to get admission. The word *scientist* stands for SC-ienti-ST. A comfortably deceiving word, *scientist* was used by the Loser Community in referring to SC/ST students in their conversation.

Achchut (untouchable), *dehati* (literally one from rural background) and *junglee* (meaning wild; used to refer to tribals whose traditional residence is in forested land) are other terms used in many college campuses to refer to SC/ST students. *Adivasi* is a formal umbrella word for all the tribal communities of India. But this word can very well be used as a slur; in such a case the word actually carries the intentional meaning an uncivilised barbarian.

This country is a rich mine of folk sayings. Many of these folk sayings ridicule and make fun of upper castes and some of these use severe expletives to do that. Of these, many are directed towards the *sahukar* and the *mahajan*, and how unscrupulously they make life of the poorer miserable. Alas while the shadow of globalisation is looming large not much attempt has been made to compile folk sayings from various regions of the country. Given the pace of global homogenisation, in less than a generation's time many folk expletives will die and will not be available for future generations. As a child I was especially fond of the village barber in my father's native place. He was a Wikipedia of folk tales, love songs, bhajans, and expletive-ridden poems. Many of these he had learnt from his father who had inherited the knowledge from his father. This hereditary transfer of skills is but common in caste system. This summer I visited the village especially to meet him and collect some gaali quotes. As I found out, he is no more and his sons, preoccupied in their own business, had not inherited the folk literature which is no longer remunerative (people prefer watching movies than going to the neighbourhood folk programme).

Other than folk literature, ridicule of upper castes is also found in street literature. A friend in Patna had once recited an interesting, albeit ugly and vulgar, poem poking Rajput haughtiness:

Garam tera khoon to garam mera moot

Lekin tu veer, mein achchut

Saale Rajput ke poot, teri maa ki chut

(If your blood is hot so is my urine

But you consider yourself brave and me untouchable

Saale son of Rajput, your mother's cunt [your Rajput heritage is no better than your mother's cunt])

Using the word nigger in US can put you in shitty trouble with the law. In India, there is no explicit codification of law of contempt pertaining to gaalis of the nature of ethnic slur. But then progressive law can go a long way in redressing these issues. Secondly, there is low awareness about the kind of damage such slurs do. Many don't even know that chinky is a slur. Hence school curriculums need to be used to sensitise students about the harmful effects of such slurs. This is one class of gaalis which is harmful if it stays in the underground. These expletives need to be brought out in the open and debated upon.

Even if we debate about the issue, you can never fully understand how much such slurs hurt unless you are the receiver of the slur. But then these slurs reinforce a sense of alienation against the society at large. Gaalis such as chinky are actually chinks in our armour, affecting social health of this nation.

Now that I think about it, I think I am fucking lucky. I am a brown Indian in free India. We always take it for granted, but it is sheer fortune that we are Indians in India. In the next chapter we will explore how it is to be an ethnic Indian in another man's land.

INSET # 4.1 SOME COMMON CASTEIST SLURS[15]

Word	Region	Remarks
Achchut	All of India	Means untouchable, used in a derogatory sense.
Bhangi	UP, Bihar, MP, Haryana	A Dalit caste. Traditional job is cleaning latrines and handling dead bodies. Bhangis are considered 'untouchable among untouchables'.
Sakkili	Sri Lanka	Sakkiliar is a Tamil Dalit caste. They are traditionally involved in removing human excrement, and hence an equivalent of Bhangi caste in the region. In Sri Lanka *Sakkili* is used as a slur on all Tamil Lankans.

Chamar	UP, Bihar, Haryana, Nepal	A Dalit caste. Traditional occupation is manufacturing and trade of leather.
Paraiya	Tamil Nadu, Kerala, Sri Lanka	A Dalit caste variously called Parayar, Sambavar, and Berava. *Paraiya* is a derivative of the now archaic word Pariah which has been adopted in English vocabulary and means an outcast. Traditionally agricultural workers; also beat drums in festivals.
Parrayande mone	Kerala	Son of a pariah.
Parrayande mole	Kerala	Daughter of a pariah.
Parachi	Tamil Nadu, Kerala, Sri Lanka	Female version of Paraiya.
Hadi Pana	Orissa	A compound of two Dalit castes of Orissa. The swearword is used for a person who stays dirty.
Chuda	Punjab, Haryana	Originally name of a Dalit caste, used as a swearword by upper caste Sikhs and Jats.
Dedh	Haryana	Used disparagingly by dominant Jats against Dalit caste men, primarily Valmiki caste members.

INSET # 4.2 ETHNIC SLURS ON MUSLIMS BY HINDUS IN VARIOUS PARTS OF THE COUNTRY[16]

Slur	Region	Meaning
Katwa	Hindi belt	Literally means someone who has been cut; alludes to removal of foreskin in a ritual involving circumcision of male children.
Landya	Maharashtra	Same as *katwa* in Marathi.
Katla loda	Gujarat	Same as *katwa* in Gujarati
Mianhchod	Gujarat	Complex of mianh (reference to Muslim word for gentleman) and chod (fuck); means one who is fucked by Muslims.
Mukaal	Tamil Nadu, Sri Lanka	Literally means three-fourth (3 4); intent same as *katwa.*
Thulukan	Tamil Nadu, Sri Lanka	Derived from the word Turk, it is used to imply that Muslims are outsiders.
Thulukan-Pundai	Tamil Nadu	More derogatory than Thulukan; 'pundai' means cunt in Tamil.
Mlechha	North India	*Mlechha* is an ethnocentric word mentioned in the Manusmriti to disparage foreigners. When used against Muslims the word indicates the foreign origin of the religion and the belief that Muslims are barbarians. The word is also used to mean that they are dirty and unholy.
Soowar, Soowar ka aulaad	UP, Bihar	*Soowar* literally means pig; *soowar ka aulaad* means 'offspring of a pig'. Soowar can be used against just anybody but Muslims find it very offensive because pigs are considered unholy.

Sulla	Himachal Pradesh, Jammu	This is a derogatory word for Muslims in Dogri speaking areas.
Turaqodu	Andhra Pradesh	Turaqodu is derived from two telugu words *turaqa* (meaning reverse) and *vadu* (meaning person). The word is used against Muslims to mean people who do reverse of what normal people do. As compared to Hindus, Muslims write from right to left, marry first cousins etc. The word is used contemptuously, making it an evidence of ethnocentrism. The word is also used to mean people from Turkey, i.e outsiders.

5

Go Back Keling

Xenophobia and slurs

Racial prejudice is a terrible thing, Yossarian. It really is. It's a terrible thing to treat a decent, loyal Indian like a nigger, kike wop or spic.

Chief Halhoat to Yossarian
in movie Catch 22

This white shit thinks he can steal my things and sell it back to me? He's got less brains than you, Lenny! Get Nick, that greasy wop, shistos, pesevengi, gamouri Greek bastard 'round 'ere now, if he's stupid enough to still be on this planet

—Rory Breaker
in Lock, stock and two smoking barrels

Globalisation is an age-old phenomenon. While developments in transport and communication in the last one century has put globalisation in a fast-track, migration has been happening in waves all through human history. The high traffic of migratory movements of last century has, however, brought peoples of different colours, manners, tones, and beliefs into a face off. A reaction to this trend is xenophobia – an antipathy towards foreigners.

However, xenophobia is not an exclusive phenomenon of our age. The early Aryans used the word *Mleccha* (pronounced in Hindi as malecch) for foreigners. The word *Mleccha* means barbarian and the *Arya* (meaning noble, civilised) used this word in a derogative manner against foreigners. There are many interesting theories about the origin of *Mleccha*[17]. The word is not found in Vedas; the first reference to *Mleccha* was in the late Vedic text *Satapatha Brahmana* which is actually part of an oral tradition dating to before 500 BC. One theory states that it is derived from the Sanskrit root *Mlech* which means to utter indistinctly. Since foreigner tongue and tone was foreign to Aryans, they found their language indistinct and thus labelled foreigners as *Mleccha*.

Yet another theory is that *Mleccha* was a language of the Indus Valley Civilisation (*Mleccha* could also have been derived from *Meluhha* which was a country Indus Valley citizens used to trade with). Since Aryans considered them inferior they attached the word to anyone foreign and barbaric. If this theory be true, irony is that Aryans were foreigners in Indian land but labelled the natives as foreigners.

Over the years, the word *Mleccha* has taken on numerous meanings. Quite early in the development of the word, it came to be associated with eating meat. The word has been used against tribal groups (especially of Central India) to mean barbaric people. Untouchable castes were also called *Mleccha* and owing to this *Mleccha* took on a new meaning: outcaste. Since untouchable castes were made to do dirty jobs, *Mleccha* also came to be associated with the word *maila* which means dirty or unholy. At one time Kushana and Saka kings were also referred to as *Mleccha.*

In contemporary times, the word has been used mostly as a derogatory label for Muslims. When used against Muslims, the word can carry any or many of the following prejudices:

- That Muslims are foreigners. This is indicative of the fall of Hindu dominance by foreign invaders who were Muslims. Implicit meaning is that Muslims do not belong to this land.
- That they are unholy and dirty people. This is because many Muslims are Hindu converts. Once a Hindu is converted, he (she) becomes unholy and *maila.*
- That they eat meat (indicative of cow meat).

While Indians have had their moments of xenophobia, it is also true that Indians have moved out to the world. Today the population of persons of Indian origin and NRIs world over is more than 24 million. This chapter seeks to briefly look into ethnic slurs that ethnic Indians are subjected to.

Button-heads

In Japan, they use the offensive word 'gaijin' for all outsiders, i.e. all people who are not Japanese. However, in most other countries there are specific slurs for visible minority communities with ethnic origin outside their country.

In Britain, the word most used to label people of South Asian origin is *Paki.* Few in USA have even heard this word, but in UK it is considered a severe racist slur. The origin from Pakistan is but obvious.

There was a big wave of immigrants from South Asia to UK in the 1950s and 1960s. At that time many tabloids used the word in a derogatory manner to refer to them as migrants from countries formerly ruled by Britain. In contemporary times Pakistanis don't take much offense from the label. However, peoples of Indian, Bangladeshi, and Afghan origin take offense from the usage of the word to label them. In a BBC research conducted in 2000, expletives were ranked on the basis of perceived severity among people of UK. Paki was ranked 10th on the basis of severity, above arse, whore, and dick but below fuck, motherfucker and nigger[18] . In the movie *Bend it like Beckham*, protagonist Jess (an Indian British) tells Joe: 'She called me a Paki. But I guess that's something you wouldn't understand'. And Joe replies 'Jess, I'm Irish. Of course I understand what that feels like'.

Yet another word which is found pretty offensive is *raghead*. The slur is used in US and UK against all those who wear a headgear. Arabs and other Middle-Eastern peoples wear headgear as part of their traditional costumes. Hence they are often the target of this abuse. In Iraq, American soldiers out there to bring peace (supposedly) term Iraqis as ragheads and Hajis. Military officers in Iraq have been reported to have cracked jokes such as 'Go kill some ragheads and burn some turbans'[19] . Sikhs also wear a headgear, which has religious significance for them. Hence members of the Sikh community are also referred to as raghead. Sikhs are also referred to as DIP – Dumb Idiotic Punjabis – in America and Canada.

Bud Bud Ding Ding is an interesting racial slur against Indians. Now this is creative; at least not as dumb as British label Paki. When I first heard about it from a friend now based in an US university, I was confused if this really is a swearword. *Bud Bud Ding Ding* actually mocks the accent of first generation migrants from India. As a slur, it should be said quickly, with a slight accent and subtle head tilting action.'[20] Another word for first generation migrants is FOB: Fresh off the Boat. This is mostly used by xenophobic US citizens who are wary of new immigrants.

There are also funny (sounds funny to me, at least) comments based on the bindi that Indian women put on forehead. Some Indian men, especially from South India, also put vermillion dots on forehead. Hence in some places in America people use words like *dothead, button-head, push-button*, and *target* (the red dot looks like a laser mark) to refer to Indians. However, these comments lack the nature of a slur. When used on ethnic Indians at max they manage to irritate or frustrate. Many of my friends in US have not heard these words. Those who have say words like *dothead* are used in local slang dialects and don't attach any negative stereotype to Indians. Rather Indians in US find the word 'Apu' more perplexing. Apu is a character in the famous *Simpsons* series. Apu is a Hindu who talks with a funny accent (an exaggeration of Indian accent), worships weird idols, and is an unscrupulous convenience store owner. To everyone who visits his shop he says "Thank you, come again". This negative stereotype has got stuck to the Indian identity in the eyes of *Simpsons* viewers. Hence ethnic Indians are subject to, mostly in a jocular sense, the Apu nick and the Thank-You-Come-Again comment. Indians however find these comments offensive and stereotypical.

The Diaspora in America and Canada consists mostly of migrants who had gone there post-independence. An earlier wave of migration happened during colonial rule under the indenture system. Under this system, many poor workers were sent to Mauritius, Fiji, Guyana, the Caribbean, and East Africa. Many others were sent to Sri Lanka, Burma, and Malaysia to work on plantations. Owing to the modest beginnings of these migrants, ethnic Indians in places like Guyana, Trinidad & Tobago, and South Africa are mocked at as coolie. Coolie is not a derisive term for Indians in India; coolie is the Hindi word for day labourers. However, in these other places Indians are now a prosperous community. The use of coolie incites the memory of their ancestors who arrived as coolies.

None of the slurs discussed afar incite as much outrage as the word *Keling* does for Indian Malaysians. It won't be an understatement to state that Keling invokes as much resentment among ethnic Indians in Malaysia as Nigger does among African Americans.

Indians constitute about 8 per cent of Malaysia's 27 million people and are the third largest ethnic group after Malays and ethnic Chinese. Indians are also poorer than Malays and Chinese. The government of Malaysia follows a policy of favouritism towards Malays, also referred to as *Bhumiputeras* (literally sons of the soil), in economic and political spheres. Owing to this and various other reasons there is friction among Malays and Indians of Malaysia. Indian community leaders have alleged that ethnic Indians are subjected to economic and cultural discrimination.

GUNGA DIN

Gunga Din is a derogatory term used for Indians in UK. It implies that Indians are subservient, that Indians are of lower status to native English. The word is derived from a poem by Rudyard Kipling written on the backdrop of colonial India. The poem tells the tale of few English soldiers fighting insurgents. An Indian servant (Gunga Din) gives up his life to protect these soldiers, thus proving his loyalty to the white colonial masters. The soldiers recite this poem in honour of Gunga Ram.

While Kipling's poem is in honour of the loyal Indian servant, the poem is actually a case of stark racism. The closing lines of this poem are:

You Lazarushian-leather Gunga Din!
Though I've belted you and flayed you,
By the livin' Gawd that made you,
You're a better man than I am, Gunga Din!

What the poem implies is that by being loyal to his English masters, Gunga Ram who is a lowly Indian has met a noble end. He is faithful to his masters in spite of being 'belted' and 'flayed'. The narrator closes the poem by magnanimously stating that even if an Indian he is better than his ruler. The poem sounds much like a master complementing his pet dog for staying by his side during his difficult times. The way we say dog is more loyal to man than another man. No wonder today Gunga Din is

In the backdrop of this political context, a marked similarity can be observed in the development of Nigger and Keling as slurs. Negro and Nigger are derivatives of the Latin word Niger which means black. This was the word used by White Americans to refer to slaves from Africa. Even after abolition of slavery African Americans (still called Nigger) were subjected to severe discrimination. It was in the backdrop of this discrimination that Nigger became an ethnic slur. 'Black' is a non-offensive racial identity but Nigger which implies the same is an offensive word. This is because the word Nigger is symbolic of a history of discrimination and deprivation.

Calling a Bihari *bihari* in Mumbai is considered offensive because of the discriminatory attitude meted out to them by people adhering to the Marathi Manoos ideology. Bud Bud Ding Ding, dothead, and Apu are just mildly offensive because these racist terms are not associated with a history of grievances. But Keling is.

Keling is derived from the word Kalinga which was a powerful empire on India's eastern coast (covering modern day Orissa). The kingdom of Kalinga had significant cultural and economic influences on South East Asia, so much so that people of the region called India *Benua Keling* and a 7th century Indonesian kingdom was named Kalingga. The *Bali* Yatra conducted every year in Cuttack city of Orissa is a tradition continuing from these ancient times. The yatra marks the onset of ships for Bali (now in Indonesia) and other places in South East Asia. The *Sejarah Melayu* (Annals of Malay History), written in 15th century traces the origin of Malay sultans to princes of Keling[21] . There are many places and monuments in Malaysia which bear the name keeling. Till as late as 1950s, Keling was not an offensive word; it just meant people from India.

With a background of discrimination, Keling soon became a

derogatory word. Today it implies that Indians are liars, untrustworthy and unscrupulous. Phrases such as *janji keling* (Indian's promise) and *cakap macam keling* ('talks like a Keling') are used by Malays to refer to liars or to those who are fickle minded and change their decision frequently. 'Go back Keling' is a phrase asking ethnic Indians to go back to India.

Broadly, ethnic slurs discussed above are of two types: those that ridicule and those that insult. Slurs that ridicule do not cause much harm beyond creating pestering stereotypes. They are a product of ethnocentrism. But the case of insults like Nigger and Keling is different; such slurs seek to trigger memories of a history of discrimination and ill-treatment.

A people may go all round the world. Their origins will still hound them. Even if they forget their origin, there are others who won't. Creating boundaries is a faster process than assimilation. When the Aryans came to India, they assimilated the natives, but so as to maintain the boundary created the concept of caste. For all we know, caste names such as *chamar* and *chandal* might have been ethnic slurs on natives in that era.

Since the people of Kalinga had gone to South East Asia and Sri Lanka centuries ago, they have been successfully assimilated with the locals. Also, they migrated not as plantation workers but as rich merchants. They had an upper hand in their dealing with locals and hence were readily accepted. But Tamil Indians, who migrated just about one or two centuries ago, have maintained their separate identity. Naturally the xenophobic natives branded them with derogatory gaalis. The way locals perceive immigrant communities is perhaps best exemplified by the Thai slur for Indians: *Kaek* which means guest. And these *kaeks* have been based in Thailand for more than two centuries.

In the light of this argument, it can be said that ethnic slurs are a symbolic expression of fear or antipathy or both (against the African slaves White Americans had antipathy; against white collar immigrants they have fear). Prejudices that may take so many words to convey are easily conveyed by slurs. Ethnic slurs are symbolic of the past and reminder for times to come. Slurs emerge out of past history of ethnic animosity and reinforce the memory of this animosity in the present and future.

INSET # 5.1 LIST OF ETHNIC SLURS AGAINST INDIANS WORLD OVER[22]

Word	Usage region	Remarks
Â châ	China	This slur is used by Cantonese speaking crowd especially those from Hong Kong and Southeast Asia. The term alludes to the frequent uttering of 'âcchâ' (Hindi अच्छा, meaning 'good, fine') by Hindi speaking people. Originally the slur was used with reference to the Punjabi 'Singh' security force employed by the British government during colonial era. Nowadays all Indians are indiscriminately called 'â châ'.
Chara	South Africa	A South African term for Indians. Not as derogatory as coolie.
Coolie	South Africa, the Caribbean	Means day labourers; refers to the fact that Indians migrated to the place as indentured labourers.
Cow-Kisser	USA	For the worship of cows in India.
Curry-Muncher	Australia, New Zealand	Indians eat Curry.
Dhoti	Nepal	The slur is used against the Madhesi people of Nepal (who are originally from Bihar) by the Nepali people.
D.I.P.	USA	Dumb Idiotic Punjab.

Dot Knot	USA	Dot (red dot on forehead) + Knot (turbins on Punjabs).
Dot/Dot-Head	USA	Refers to the "bindi" (dot) on Indian women's foreheads.
Gas Pumper	USA	Many gas stations are owned and operated by Indians. Hence the nick.
Gunga Din	UK	Based on a character named Gunga Din developed by Rudyard Kipling who was a loyal servant in the army in British India. The word is used derogatorily to imply that Indians are subservient to the English.
Higger	USA	Hindus who act Black.
Indonigger	USA	Indian who acts like a Black, or is darker in skin.
Julab	USA	Means "wet shit" in Hindi/Punjabi
Kaek	Thailand	Thais, living in Thailand, refer to ethnic Indians (who have been in Thailand for at least 200 years) as Kaeks, which means "guest" in Thai.
Kala	Myanmar (Burma)	Literally means foreigner; used for Indians who have been in Myanmar now for over two centuries.
Mahout	New York (USA)	Literally means "Elephant Driver" but was turned into a popular racial slur around 1997 when a lot of Indains began to move onto Long Island.
Mama	Singapore	'Mama' literally means uncle in Tamil. 'Mama stalls' are cheap, convenience stores typically run by Indians in Singapure. The slur comes from here.
Mingita	UK	Used for lesbian Indian women. The word is offensive.
Nigdu	USA	Nigger + Hindu. Half black, half Indian. Also means an Indian who behaves like a black.

Paki	UK	Short for Pakistani. Often not derogatory when used. In The UK many Indians and Pakistanis have been lumped under the same term. It's much more of a slur to Indians
Pariah	Singapore, Malaysia, Sri Lanka	Paraiya is a low caste in India and pariah is a derivative of the caste name meaning an outcaste. The word pariah is used on Indians in mock (as well as in disgust) in Singapore and Malaysia to imply that Indians discriminate against outcastes in their society when they are no better.
Push-Button / Push-start	USA	Refers to the *bindi* on Indian women's foreheads.
Raghead	USA, UK	Directed at people who use traditional headdress, such as Arabs and Sikhs.
Reset	USA	The word comes from the red dot on Indian women's forehead (bindi) which resembles the reset button on many electronic gadgets.
Sakkili	Sri Lanka	Sakkiliar is a low caste in Tamil community of Sri Lanka, considered dirty and filthy. Lankans use the word to refer to all Tamils.
Target	USA	The dot on Indian women's head looks like a laser sight.
Turbinator	USA	Sikh Indians because of their religious custom of wearing turbans.
Wog	UK	Used by British imperialists to refer to Indians as they were the personal security guards. It stands for "Warden on Guard".
Yìndù â sân	China	'â' is a vocative, and 'sân' is three, so 'â sân' means the third son or third child in a family. The slur indicates that Yìndùs (Hindus, referring to Indians in general) have third-class status in China.

6

Mader, not Fader

The sociology of gaalis

Soap: Oh, you assume, do you? And what did I say about assumptions being the brother of all fuck-ups?
Tom: It's the *mother* of all fuck-ups, stupid!
Soap: Well, brother, mother, or any other sucker! It don't make any difference. They're still fucking guns and they still fire fucking bullets!

—In the movie Lock, stock and two smoking barrels

The nature and preponderance of swearwords in a language ultimately depends on the society in which people speak this tongue. The patterns and features of society cast a shadow on what is and what is not offensive in language. After all, taboo is a fiction created by society. So also are stereotyping of ethnic groups.

What constitutes taboo in one society need not be taboo in another. As a consequence of this, what constitutes swearword in one society may not be considered offensive in another. In America, only ten taboo words account for over 80 per cent of swearwords used by the common man. These are *fuck, shit, hell, damn, goddamn, Jesus Christ, ass, oh my God, bitch*, and *sucks*[23]. Of these, you won't be able to find any equivalent for *goddamn* or *Jesus Christ* in Indian gaali vocabulary. '*Hey Ram*' can be considered an equivalent of *Oh my God*; but 'hey Ram' is not a gaali. In fact, the last words Mahatma Gandhi uttered before his death were 'hey Ram'. His memorial at Raj Ghat also bears this epigraph.

While the psychological bases of swearwords and their utility can be generalised across cultures, wide cross-cultural variations exist in the nature of swearwords actually used by peoples. To understand this we need to analyse particular societies. In Christianity, taking the name of God without any reason is a blasphemy. A verse from the Bible clearly mentions that:

> Thou shalt not take the name of the LORD thy God in vain; for the LORD will not hold him guiltless that taketh his name in vain (Exodus 20:7)[24]

Hence words like *Jesus Christ* and *Oh my God* are taboo. On the other hand, there is no such concept of blasphemy in Hinduism. In fact Hinduism adheres to numerous philosophies that take varied (and often contradictory) stand. There are schools of thought that believe in God and schools that don't (for example, the *nastika* school). Further, the various branches of Hindu religion practised in India 'did not possess a well-ordered set of commandments or do's and don'ts.'[25] God existed in countless forms and each manifestation had a different personality; each divine personality had numerous human characteristics. As a result it is not easy to compress 'blasphemous references to god or the devil, in a succinct swear word.'[26] On the contrary, it is considered pious to take the name of Gods. My grandmother recites hundred-and-eight names of Lord Shiva daily in the morning. She holds a string of beads in her hand so that she does not lose count. It is believed that when your life nears its end you should keep reciting names of Gods all through the day, so as to be reborn a good creature.

In stark contrast to the West, the gaalis predominantly used in Hindi heartland are:

1. *Harami*
2. *Saala*
3. *Kamina*
4. *Maderchod/ maachod*
5. *Behenchod*
6. *Lowda*
7. *Gaand mar* and
8. *Chutiya*[27]

An equivalent of motherfucker and sister fucker can be found in most societies, modern and ancient. This is perhaps because, as famous psychoanalyst Sigmund Freud had reasoned, incest and patricide are the only two universal taboos. Incest being taboo in every society, its projection in cuss words can be found in most societies. However, some societies use the M-word and S-word more frequently while others use it rarely.

East is East and West is West, so they say. While as many as five of the most used swearwords in American vocabulary are blasphemous, bastard (*harami*), motherfucker (*maderchod*), and sisterfucker (*behenchod*) don't find a mention. This has been puzzling me for quite some time now. To crack this puzzle we need to dive deep into lineaments of Indian society.

Indian patriarchy

Indian society is predominantly a patriarchal society. In traditional patriarchy, there is stringent division of labour between the sexes – men work outside the house and women do all work within the household. As a result, men are seen to contribute all income earned by the family. When a girl is born in such a patriarchy, she finds differential treatment meted out to her and her brothers. Her brothers are pampered by mother because they are seen as independent resources who would grow up to earn for the family. Logically she should rebel because of the discriminatory attitude of her mother. But that is not so[28] . On the contrary she internalises the belief that men are *independent resources* where as women are dependent on men for a good life. She indulges her brother the way her mother does. At the same time she makes the brother realise that she needs to be protected – that she is dependent on him.

This expectation is best exemplified by festivities like *raksha bandhan*. The root purpose of *raksha bandhan* is to remind the brother that he should protect her. Hence the expectation from a man to protect his sister's honour is embedded in social values. When someone swears *saala* at a brother, he basically provokes the brother's ability to protect his sister's honour. *Saala* literally means wife's brother. But when you use it as a swearword you mean you sleep with the receiver's sister. If I call you *saala* (no offence intended) I basically mean that you are my woman's brother. Since I am not married to your sister, *saala* simply implies that I have illicit sexual relation with your sister. Such a gaali is supposed to challenge your ability to protect your sister's honour – your *mardangi*[29] (manlihood).

Gaalis like *behenchod*, *behen ka lowda* and *behen de takey* are also intended to provoke the receiver. *Behenchod* is the most severe of these gaalis because it implies that you yourself violate your sister's honour.

When this girl marries, she enters her new household as a *bahu*(daughter-in-law), not wife. Psychoanalyst Sudhir Kakar reasons that at this stage the *bahu* does not have any status in the new family[30] . Her *saas* (mother-in-law) feels threatened by her presence. The *saas* had nurtured her son with extreme indulgence with the intention of being the most important woman in his life. The *bahu* is a threat because she can radically influence the son with her youthful sexuality. As one scholar observes,

Since sons are a woman's most critical resource, ensuring their life-long loyalty is an enduring preoccupation. Older women have a vested interest in the suppression of romantic love between youngsters to keep the conjugal bond secondary and to claim sons' primary allegiance[31]

As a result, the *bahu* is marginalised in this new family she has joined. She has the lowest status in family hierarchy, and she realises that she needs a 'loyal man' of this family to help her rise in family hierarchy.

She finds this loyal man when she becomes the mother of a male child. Even though a *bahu*, she was still an outsider. But now that she has given birth to a male member of the patriarchy, she is very much an insider. Not only is she grateful to this male child, this child also happens to be the pinnacle of her achievement: she has created a male member of the family. Grateful that she is, she over-indulges this child[32] . Not only is she madly in love with her son, she also vocally expresses her love for him. There are a hundred names by which my mother calls me... I am her baby, also her Kanha (that's how Yashodha called her son Krishna), also her *dhana* (wealth), also the most handsome creature in this world.

Owing to this indulgence, the mother-son attachment is especially strong in Indian society. Mother-son relationship is glorified, and many literary writings, mythologies, and folk songs also indicate that the mother is the most important person in a man's life. The son also realises that he is the protector of his mother, and if he is a real man (has *mardangi*) he will protect her honour. So to hurt a man real bad, one has to swear at his mother, not him. '*Teri Maa Ki...*', literally 'Your mother's...' is the beginning of a sentence that could be any insult to the receiver's mother. For example *Teri Maa Ki Aankh* means 'Your mother's vagina' (*aankh* literally means eyes but is used here as euphemism for vagina). Very often just the words *Teri Maa Ki* evoke deep sentiments in the receiver.

Maderchod is the most severe gaali you can inflict on an Indian man, because it alleges that he has himself violated the honour of his mother.

Teri Maa Ki...	
Teri maa ka bhosda	Your mother's breasts
Teri maa ki chut	Your mother's cunt
Teri maa ki aankh	Your mother's eyes/vagina
Maa ke laude	Mother's dick
Maa ke tatte	Mother's balls
Kutte ke poot, teri maa ki chut	Son of a dog, your mother's cunt
Maa ke dale	Mother's pimp
Maa ke bhadwe	Mother's pimp

Teri maa gandi randi	Your mother is a filthy whore
Teri maa ki phudi gai ki hai	Your mother has a cow's cunt
Teri maa ki bimaar badbudar choot	Your mother's diseased smelly cunt
Teri maa ki chut me mera land	My dick in your mother's cunt

Table 6.1 Some common gaalis insulting the receiver's mother

Purity & sexuality

Virginity is a big deal in India. It still is. While a burden for boys, virginity is seen as a virtue in girls. A guy may graze around butting himself in at every possible opportunity of getting carnal pleasure still he would search for a virgin for marriage. This is because traditionally female sexuality is deeply linked to purity. A 'pure woman' (*pavitra naari*) is one who has had sex with just one man, the man she has been wedded to with sanction of society.

Some sociologists trace the origin of purity-sexuality linkage to a characteristic feature of Indian society: caste. Caste system itself is a fiction created by society to imply that different people have different statuses because they are differently pure. There is a frustrated looking old man with three heads and a young, beautiful chick as wife in Indian mythology and supposedly all humans have originated from this oldie. What differentiates people is how they have originated. If you have originated from his head you are purest, if from his feet the least pure, and if from his dick... well, eh ... I don't know; this oldie himself looks like a diseased dick with severe erectile dysfunction, so if you are a Hindu you have anyways originated from a dick.

Hence all castes are organised in the form of a hierarchy with the purest castes on top and the most polluted at the bottom of the hierarchy. So as to maintain its ritual purity, every caste has to ensure that inter-marriage with lower castes does not happen. If a member of a Brahmin caste (higher ritual purity), for example, marries a member of Chamar caste (lower ritual purity) the offspring is less pure than a Brahmin but is still part of the Brahmin family; hence he becomes a threat to the myth of castes.

The *manusmriti* however sanctions certain forms of inter-caste marriage. After marrying a woman of the same caste (*savarna* marriage or endogamy), a man may marry women of lower castes. This is called *anuloma* (hypergamy). Yet, *pitriloma* (hypogamy) – marriage of a woman of higher caste to a man of lower caste – is not allowed. *Manusmriti* states that marriage between a Brahmin woman and a Shudra man is the gravest of all sins. The offspring of such an union is a Chandal. This implies that castes usually attach a greater degree of purity to purity of their women. As one sociologist observes:

> Historically the development of Hindu society has been one of ever increasing hierarchy –of hierarchy based explicitly on an ideology of a parallel development of institutions concerned with the control of female sexuality…[whenever] purity is the primary idiom of status differentiation, there is certain to be a major preoccupation with the maintenance of female chastity. This is especially so in India where the purity of the caste is a direct function of the purity of its womenfolk. The male members of the caste are in large measure dependant for their status rating on the purity of their women.[33]

This concept of female sexuality as symbol of purity/pollution is also exemplified in many mythologies and folk tales. In the Ramayana, for example, Ravana kidnaps Sita and keeps her for fourteen years at his palace in Lanka. Rama attacks Lanka because it was a challenge to his *mardangi*, to the honour of his royal patriarchy. Yet he does not accept Sita when Lanka falls. This is because Sita had become impure. Thereafter Sita gets the testimony of fire God to convince Rama that she's still pure. But the people of Ayodhya are not convinced that after fourteen long years Sita remains pure. Under the pressure of public outcry Rama eventually excommunicates Sita from his kingdom.

In stark contrast, Helen of Troy was kidnapped by Theseus when she was quite young. After that she was married to Menelaus the brother of Agamemnon. Some versions of the story imply that she had sexual relations with Agamemnon too. Later she elopes with Paris of Troy and becomes his wife. The Trojan War continues for ten long years, and Paris dies sometime in between. Then she marries Deiphobus, Paris' brother. After Troy was conquered by Greek forces, Menelaus again reclaims her. This is a story Indian audiences will find funny and hard to correlate.

Virginity as purity and one-man-woman as virtuous woman are deeply embedded in Indian society. It is in fact religious censorship which has, through institutions like caste, 'placed the main onus of maintaining the sanctity and purity of everything' on women. This again is a major reason why gaalis such as *saala*, *maa ke dalle* are widely used. *Sasura* and *sasur ke naati* are two widely used euphemisms in Hindi heartland of East UP and West Bihar. *Sasura* technically means father-in-law. But if I address you as *sasura* I basically mean that I sleep with your daughter. This gaali is so popular in this region because a man's honour lies in his daughter's purity. *Sasur ke naati* literally means father-in-law's grandson, i.e. wife's son. When used as swear, it means implies that the gaali-giver sleeps with the receiver's mother.

The father in patriarchy

While the honour of the women in a patriarchal set up carries high value, it is eventually men who constitute the patriarchy. One derives his primary social identity from his family, and his family gets its identity from its male head – his father or grandfather. The very common gaali *harami* (also *haramkhor*) literally means bastard, one who is the product of an illicit sexual relationship. It is derived from Urdu word haramzada; *haram* in Persian means illegal and *zada* means product. While bastard is not a popular cuss word in Western societies, *harami* is in India. This is because a man derives social status from his family and caste. The legitimacy of a person as a son of his father is the only means for him to gain membership of his father's caste and kin network.

"The father is undoubtedly the most important member of the family. The sole breadwinner, he is the solid bedrock upon which the entire family is built. The family, each of its members, derives expression, identity, from the central father figure: without him the whole structure breaks down, dissolves to nothingness. The *honour* of the family is reflected in his person and conduct; further, as the only link between the microcosmic family and the macrocosmic society, his role as the 'protector' is of prime importance."[34]

This makes *harami* a common gaali to offend a person in India.

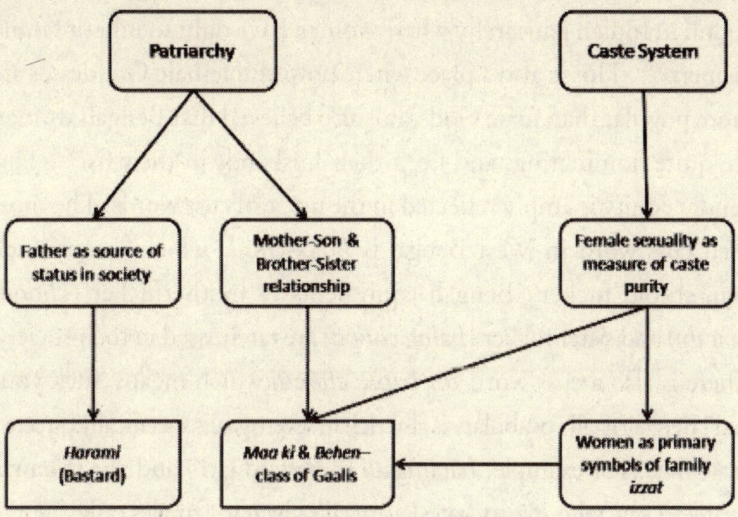

Figure 6.1 Sociological causation of major gaalis

A common feature of gaalis discussed in this chapter till now is that the gaalis are directed at the honour – the *izzat* – of the receiver. Whether referring to illicit sexual relations of female relations or doubting the family name, these gaalis imply that the receiver has no *izzat* in society. One gaali that directly points to a person's *izzat* is *kamina* (plural *kaminey*). *Kamina* is derived from the Persian word *Kameen* which means 'a lowly person'. *Kamina* means a person who has no *izzat*, is deceitful, unreliable, and shameless. This gaali roughly corresponds to the English swear rascal.

Whither Dah-Bei?

An interesting trend in the usage of gaali is observed as you move eastward from Central India. Bengali society has traditionally given greater respect to its women than the Hindi belt. Bengal is the only region in Indian patriarchy where women have right to inherit family property[35] . This is also a place where powerful female Goddesses are more popular than male Gods. It is also believed that Bengali women are quite dominating, and keep their husbands in their fist[36] . This gender equity is amply reflected in the usage of cuss words. The most used cuss word in West Bengal is *boka-choda* which means 'fuck you, stupid fucker'. Bengali equivalents of motherfucker (*chood-marani*) and sister fucker (*baing chood*) are rarely used in their society. There is also a cuss word *tor bapre choodi* which means 'fuck your dad'! Bengali gaali vocabulary is also rich in severe gaalis specifically directed at women. For example, *haramgadi* ('a bastard girl') and *sut-marawni* (wanker/ one who masturbates) are gaalis given to females only.

Moving further east we see that Assam is the frontier region of the patriarchal belt. The most used cuss (and the only cuss frequently used) in Assamese is *kela* which means dick. All the states surrounding Assam have tribal societies in which gender disparity is generally low. In fact, the *Khasi*s and *Garo*s of Meghalaya have matriarchal family structure. The mother is the theoretical head in a Khasi family. When a man marries, he comes to live with his wife at his mother-in-law's residence. It is he who pays a bride price (dowry) for the marriage. Ritual property of a woman is inherited by his youngest daughter.

Comparing matriarchal Khasis with the patriarchal belt will make a good analysis for the purpose of understanding gaalis as projection of society. Towards this purpose I interviewed few men when in Shillong, and came to know that *Eegor* ('dick') is the most used gaali in Shillong. Motherfucker (*dah-bei*) sounds funny, odd, and repulsive to a *Khasi* but it is not a cuss that the receiver finds offensive. This is because women have a strong presence in Khasi society. They are not seen as a weaker gender in need of protection from their men. Secondly, ritual purity is in no way linked to sexuality. Pre-marital sex and widow remarriage are both allowed in Khasi society.

In the ultimate analysis, the nature of Indian swearwords can be traced back to religion. Swearwords are a form of expression against censorship. There can be no swearword without censorship and censorship has no meaning in a hypothetical society with no taboos. The earliest form of censorship was religious censorship. In Western societies, *damn*, *Goddamn*, and *Jesus Christ* were severe swearwords because swearing these was censored by the powerful Church as an act of blasphemy. These swearwords came to popular usage because they became a reaction to Papal censorship.

In an Indian context, owing to a multiplicity of (1) Gods, (2) God forms, (3) avatars, (4) divine authority, (5) religious beliefs, and (6) practices, there was no direct religious censorship. Without censorship, no swearword could develop. However, religious censorship did contribute to prevalence of other swearwords. Swearwords demeaning chastity and purity of women are a reaction to censorship by patriarchal authority as well as to caste censorship. And caste is a fiction of society legitimised by religion. Just like the Church is the institutional form of religion in Western societies, caste was the institutional form of religious sanction in Indian society.

INSET 6.1 'TERI MAA KI' CLASS GAALIS IN SOME INDIAN LANGUAGES

	Gaali	English translation
Bengali	*Tor mar doshti buni*	Your mother has ten tits
	Chude maranir pola	Son of a motherfucker
	Tor maayer gudei tel diye torr baaper bichir boda bhaajbo	I'll put some cooking oil in your mother's cunt and fry your father's balls in it
Dogri	*Maa-iyevia*	Motherfucker
	Teri madi seri	Your mother's cunt
Gujarati	*Teri ma meri lolli chatte che*	Your mum is sucking my dick
	Teri ma meri ghare nakri fara che	Your mum is walking naked in my house
	Kutri no chokroo	Son of dog
	Taari ma ni ghand	Your mom's ass
	Taari ma ni bhosri sukaygayu	Your mother's pussy dried up
	Taari ma ni bhosri machli jevi gundhai	Your mom's pussy smells like fish
	Taari ma no piko mare	Fuck your mother's cunt
	Taari Ma Ni Ghand Ma Kutra Ugge	Dogs shit in your mom's ass
	Taari maa ne mota kaarda kutra chodey	Your mum gets fucked by fat black dogs
	Theri ma ne chodyav	Go fuck your mum
	Hoo tari ma ne hathi na danda thi thokiss	I'll fuck your mother with an elephant's cock
	Tare ma na bagal ma hathi na baal	Your mum has elephant hairs in her armpits!
	Tari ma kisskoli ne gan chate!	Your mum licks a squirrel's ass!
	Tari ma fudhi maa marchu bhusee!	Your mum rubs chili powder up her pussy
	Taari maa ne moto piko ane lund che	Your mum has a big fanny and a big dick
	Tare ma na pudha meh padhu	I fart in your mother's fanny.
	Tari ma na gand ma mail man ni chavi kovai guy che	The mail man has lost his keys in your mom's pussy.

	Kutri na petna	One who has come out of a bitch's womb.
	Tari ma na gand ma moto haati no lund che	There is a big elephant dick up your mom's ass.
	Tari ma ni gaand ma garam thel bhari ne ander samosa banawu bhosidina!	May I fill your mother's ass with hot oil and fry samosas in it, you pussy!
	Tari maa ni bhosrini kutra ni lund jevi dekhai	Your mom's pussy looks like a dog's dick
Kannada	*Neen thayan haadha*	Your grandmother's cunt
	Nim avvun thullu	Your mother's cunt
	Nin amman tullu naa keya	I will fuck your mother's cunt
	Sulle magane	Son of a whore
Marathi	*Tuzya aaila puchchi*	Your mother's cunt
	Tuzya aaila zavala	Fuck your mother
	Tujhya aaila jhawla kutra	Your mother gets fucked by dogs
	Tuzhya aaila zhawla kaowla	Your mother gets fucked by crows
	Tujha aaichi gaand	Your mother's arse
	Randichya	Son of a whore
	Tuzya aaichya bhokat bhulla	My dick in your mother's cunt
	Aaila ghoda laagla	Horse fucks your mother
	Aaichya puchit pay	My legs in your mother's pussy
	Tuzhya aaichi pucchi takli	Your mother's pussy is bald
Nepali	*Tero ama ko puti*	Your mother's pussy
	Malie tero amma ko lash lai chikke	I fucked your mum's dead body
	Hijo rati maile tero amma ra bau dutai lia chike	Last night I fucked your mum and your dad
Oriya	*To bou ku gehen*	Fuck your mother
	To bou ra bia re mo banda	My dick in your mother's cunt
	Maagian	Motherfucker

Punjabi	*Teri ma di bingi lund*	Your mother's crooked dick
	Teri maa di fuddi	Your mother's cunt
	Teri maa di naas	Your mother's cunt
	Tere lan tere bebe de pudhe vich	Shove your dick into your mother
	Tere maa mera phani chat de	Your mother licks my cum
	Teri ma de lund naal gobi jamdi	— grows in your mother's dick
	Tera binga lulla teri manh di andhi fuddi vich	Your crooked dick is in your mother's smelly pussy
	Keerian Teri Maa Di Phudi Vich Varjaan	May ants infest your mother's pussy
	Tari mao ni pudhi mara	Bang your mother's pussy
	Teri ma dee gundi gatchi	Your mom's dirty underwear

7

Oh Shit!

A study in scatology

I have to admit that things are really starting to look up for me since my life turned to shit

Seymour

in Ghost World

Normally, both your asses would be dead as fucking fried chicken, but you happen to pull this shit while I'm in a transitional period so I don't wanna kill you, I wanna help you. But I can't give you this case, it don't belong to me. Besides, I've already been through too much shit this morning over this case to hand it over to your dumb ass

—Lance

in *Pulp Fiction*

There are myriad factors by which the human species creates

differences within itself – race, caste, class, gender, religion, region to name a few. In the midst of these differences there are but a few similarities that bind us together; that make us all humans. One of these is the act of defecation. Every human takes a shit once in a while. Be he a bourgeoisie with a palatial toilet or a proletariat with just the slum bowel-pot at his disposal; be he a priest or a non-believer; a soldier of holy Jehad or an anti-terrorist commando; Brahmin or Chamar; everyone shits. Shitting is human nature.

In the course of my research I was able to get hold of a chap who has sources in the White House. To my utter shock, I found that the present Black Democrat president of US of A Barack Obama shits the same colour shit that his White Republican predecessor did. It is a yellowish brown semisolid with mucus coating. What really shocked me is that they have the same colour stool as mine. I wonder if there is any similarity in stool aroma of the three of us.

Ironically, even though everyone shits, words like shit and crap drive in strongly repulsive imagery in people. And that's why such words are taboo in certain social situations. For example, it's a strict no-no to talk about shit when someone is having food around you. Defecation is not explicitly named in most social occasions. Rather terms like 'let me freshen up' and 'let me lighten up' are used.

Legend has it that when General Pervez Musharraf became president of Pakistan, the first thing that he did was order his top scientists to design a machine that would use vacuum cleaner technology to insert a pipe into soldiers' anus and take out their bodily wastes. This way his soldiers would be relieved from seeing faeces at times of frustration.

This was an attempt at reducing the stress level of on-field soldiers. Just when the machine was ready for deployment in the military, an advisor suggested that this machine would have detrimental effect if a war breaks out with India. While Indian soldiers would make Pakistani Prisoners of War eat their shit, Pakistani soldiers could not retaliate; no third degree treatment could match making an enemy soldier eat your shit. Ultimately the multimillion dollar project was dropped.

Ok, I am taking too much latitude with you. One should never shit on his readers, or if he does it should not be obvious.

Hagga

Hagga is Hindi for shit, while *hag diya* and *hagna* are Hindi words for the act of defecation. A perplexing issue in the study of Hindi swearwords is that *hagga* and its derivatives are rarely used in colloquial conversation, if at all. *Hag diya* may be used in slang dialects to imply that someone has messed up. But the usage of this word is also quite low.

One may argue that we Indians are more averse to *hagga* than our western counterparts; hence shit should be a stronger taboo here than in West. After all it is we who wash our arse after having a shit. Even some disillusioned foreigners who come to India in search of Eastern spiritualism and *moksha* go out to the fields, lota in hand, to defecate under the wide open sky and cleanse the self (arse is symbolic of the soul, *atman*) with water from the lota.

But then this is a flawed viewpoint. India is the land of shits. It has not only the second largest human population, but also the largest bovine population in the world. Everyday millions of humans and cattle defecate on the surface of Mother India. Cows being sacred to us, we let them wander around and defecate at will. It is hard to find more than a dozen Indians who have not once stepped on cow dung in their life.

Defecation is also an occasion for social gathering in India. Men of various ages would squat together by the road or rail lines shitting while they smoke bidis and wave at passing trains. Important political issues – both local and national – are discussed during these daily defecation congregations. Not only is public opinion shaped, planning for agitations and social movements are also made in these congregations. In villages this is one of the few opportunities housewives get for outing. Restricted that they are to the four walls, moving out in groups for defecation congregation in the fields is like a daily picnic.

In the movie *Slumdog Millionaire*, the child protagonist falls into a pit of human faeces, yet does not mind the yellow fluid as he comes out of the pit to meet his favourite hero. Indeed, the general prevalence of dirt in residential habitats such as slums has given rise to deprivation tourism, wherein foreigners come to slums and are awed by the ability of humans to stay in such conditions. For them it is a wonder.

While the condition in slums is explainable by high population density of individuals from low income group, it is tough to explain the general lack of civic sense in India. What can explain the pan and gutka spits in every public utility building? And the strong urine stench on corners? Prof. Dipankar Gupta from Jawaharlal Nehru University reasons that this behaviour has a close relation to caste consciousness[37]. Traditionally there have been cleaning castes in India; castes which hereditarily engage in the job of cleaning public places. We tend to keep our house (and our selves) clean because it ensures our purity. But we take no responsibility to keep public places clean, for this is someone else's job: a lower caste's job.

Hence, there is a contradiction of sorts in Indian psyche related to cleanliness. While we take it upon us to keep our private environs clean, we would rather tolerate dirt in public environs than make an effort to keep them clean. Since you walk, smoke, chew pan, litter, and pee in dirty public spaces *hagga* does not evoke a strongly repulsive imagery within you. Hence the absurdity of using *hagga* as a gaali.

Secondly, the popularity of a gaali depends to a significant extent on its usage in college campuses. Many gaalis have arisen in campus cultures while many others have fallen into disuse because college masses stop using it (in short, the gaali goes out of fashion). A gaali on dirtiness could not evolve in India perhaps because of the critical role dirt and shit play in Indian campuses. Shit is part of customary socialisation of a fresher (also called ragging) in campus. One of the most popular ragging activities is 'brain wash', in which a senior shits into a shit-pot, then a fresher is made to put his head inside the pot while someone presses the flush button.

In IIT Kharagpur, ragging was banned after a fresher died in 1992. Institute authorities severely came down upon those involved in ragging; anti-ragging squads composed of junior professors still make surprise raids on hostels. Prior to 1992 Kharagpur was infamous for having the worst ragging in Indian colleges. Currently ragging is going on in a regulated manner, and under a less controversial name: Orientation Program. One of the ragging rituals still being followed in my hall is taking a dip in a 'shit tank'. A shit tank is a tank full of stale water (as old as a month or two). However, prior to 1992 a shit tank actually contained human faeces. A fresher had to strip himself, then take a dip in this shit tank and recite the hall anthem. I am told that such rituals are still rampant in many colleges.

Freud's Hagga

A more psychological explanation for the lack of shit-equivalents in Hindi comes from Freudian theory. Sigmund Freud had theorised that a man's brain has two processors: *Id* and *Superego.* Id is instinctive and hedonistic. It is only concerned with immediate satiation of desires. Superego, on the other hand, is moralistic and induces the individual to show self-restraint. Every action of the individual is the result of a tussle between Id and Superego. Suppose you meet an irresistible girl in a party. She is irresistible because your Id feels that you should bounce on her and chew her apart. Yet you control yourself, because you know there are some social norms on propriety and acceptable behaviour. This control is governed by Superego.

Superego develops in interaction with society. You would not be born with an in-built knowledge of social norms; hence Superego does not exist at birth. It is only the Id that exists at birth. Hence, an infant has no inhibitions. That's the reason why an infant pees and defecates at will. Freud had reasoned that the development of Superego happens in stages. As parents train kids, they learn self-control. The first stage of self-control is the *oral stage*, followed by *anal stage.* In the anal stage, family elders give 'toilet training' whereby the child learns to control his bowel movements. If not given toilet training, a man would shit anywhere anytime he feels like. During toilet training the kid is taught to show dislike towards bodily wastes and trained to dispose them off at the right place. It is because of this aversion taught to the child during anal stage that bodily wastes – faeces, urine, spittle, and phlegm – become taboo (note that remarks like 'I spit on your face' or 'I will urinate all over you' are insulting)

Now coming to Indian society, toilet training in Indian families is significantly different from how it is in the West. Toilet training starts at around the age of two in Western societies. In India, however, it starts when the infant is just about three months old and continues till he/she is five years old[38]. But since a three month old cannot possibly go to a toilet and defecate there, toilet training is very liberal and lenient. The infant is taught to control bowel movement for some time till the mother takes him out to of the kitchen (or *puja* room). Till he is five years old the child has freedom to defecate anytime anywhere in the open and the faithful mother cleans it for him. I have seen young cousins defecate in the veranda, near house entrance, and even sometimes in bedrooms; yet they were not reprimanded by their indulgent mothers[39]. It is only when they turn five that they are asked to make a habit of using the toilet or go out to the fields.

In my opinion, people in India do not develop a strong childhood aversion towards faeces due to this long association with bodily wastes. Toilet training is the critical period when aversion towards faeces gets strongly embedded in a man's autonomic responses. Hence stool is not a strong taboo in India. Thence no Hindi synonym of shit could develop into a gaali.

Ghinastic

While a common gaali related to filth or shit is yet to evolve in colloquial Hindi vocabulary, localised gaalis pertaining to same are in existence. One such gaali is *ghinastic*. Ghinastic is derived from the hindi word *ghinauna* meaning disgusting (or unpleasant) and the English word nasty. Hence it's a truly Hinglish gaali. This gaali can be used to express disgust towards any filthy place or person. For instance, suppose you don't take a bath for a week or so you start smelling like a rotten fish. It is then that a friend can call you a 'ghinastic person'. If a person wears shabby dress and has not had a haircut or shave for a long time then too he can be labelled ghinastic.

> Ghinastic = Ghinauna + Nasty
>
> Ghinauna (Hindi) = Disgusting, unpleasant
>
> Nasty (English) = Dirty, offensive matter

The origin of the gaali is not clear, although one can state with reasonable accuracy that the word originated in East UP-Bihar region. Also being a soft gaali, girls find it comfortable to utter it. The gaali is also popularly spoken in coaching centres (for engineering entrance exams) of Uttar Pradesh-Bihar-Jharkhand region, which explains how students of geographically diverse campuses such as NIT Allahabad, IIT Powai, and NIT Nagpur are familiar with the gaali.

However, I doubt if ghinastic can become a popular swearword. *Shit* and *crap* are popular swearwords because these words can be used in different contexts to achieve different meanings[40]. In comparison ghinastic has a narrow meaning and narrow applicability.

This is perhaps the reason why with increased usage of English in day-to-day speak shit itself has become a common swearword in Indian gaali lexicon.

8

Homo Hierarchus

Anal sex, oral sex, and symbolism in gaalis depicting same

You see, this profession is filled to the brim with unrealistic motherfuckers. Motherfuckers who thought their ass would age like wine. If you mean it turns to vinegar, it does. If you mean it gets better with age, it don't

—Marsellus
in Pulp Fiction

The greatest monarch on the proudest throne is obliged to sit upon his own arse

—Benjamin Franklin

I don't remember the date now. Not even which year it happened. But when the first F-grade of my academic life was looming large on my neck it felt real bad.

‘You got to pay a price for acting smart with a professor’ said a fellow LLB. We, the ones whose gaands were on the line of fire, were sitting depressed in the very same classroom this professor used for his lectures.

‘Some of you may be spared. But the professor sure is getting into my gaand’ said another. From where I sat the classroom looked empty. After all it was only the LLB – League of Last Benchers – who had been given adverse grades in practicals. All through the semester it seemed so cool making commotion, cracking jokes, coming late to class. The professor looked kind and lenient and we took all latitude we got. Guys envied and girls adored, the class was an audience for the LLBs – Lords of Last Benches. Good that the audience was absent when I sat there with a bamboo in my gaand, so big that it may prop out of my mouth anytime.

‘If some may be spared why then is he greasing everyone’s gaand?’ JP wondered loud.

‘That’s not the point. He has already got into our gaands. The question is how far he is going into whose gaand and how long is he going to stay’.

‘I am sure he has a small dick’ someone said.

‘Doesn’t matter. He will stick a rail line up your gaand’.

‘And make a train run over it’.

‘Am sure that would rip your gaand apart’.

‘JP won’t feel a thing’ said JP’s roommate whose composure in these adverse times was a comfort.

‘Why so?’

‘My pappu has been practicing on his gaand. Night on night. All night’.[41]

His words instantly lightened the mood. Gaand-class of gaalis is perhaps the most humorous of Hindi gaalis. Gaand is Hindi for arse. *Gaandu* roughly corresponds to the English swearword bugger. Literally gaandu means someone who gets his arse sodomized, but is used to refer to a person as idiot. But then gaandu is a less frequently used word, used mostly by girls for guys. In a man-to-man talk, the popular cusswords are *gaand marna* and *gaand phadna*.

Gaand marna means fuck-in-the-ass. In a friendly conversation, you may tell your friend in mock affection:

'*Gaand marwaega?*'

(Will you get your ass fucked by me?)

Or with mock rage you may state:

'*Gaand maar lunga teri!*'

(I will fuck you in the ass)

Now it can get much more creative:

'*Tu jis-jis-se **gaand marwata** hai, un sabki mein maarta hun*'.

(I fornicate all those [in the ass] who fornicate you in the ass)

If a colleague is detained by the boss till late after office hour, you may wonder:

'*Us chutiye se **gaand mara** raha tha kya? Ya uska gaand chat raha tha?*'

(Were you getting fucked by the idiot in the ass or were you licking his ass [to be in his good books]?)

If in a party everyone is pulling your leg, you can put that to rest by wondering in mock frustration:

'*Mera hi gaand mila hai maarne ke liye?*'

(You people have got only my ass to fornicate?)

Gaand phadna means blast-your-ass and is a less frequently used word, mostly as an exclamation on one's own condition. For example, if girlfriend no.1 wants to go on an outing while you are with no.2, you tell her by way of an excuse:

'*Babe, gaand phati padi hai. Boss ne bahut kaam de diya.*'

(Babe, my ass has burst since the boss has given lot of work to do)

Asshole *vs* Gaand

The arse as a body part is a verbal taboo in Western societies because of its connection with another taboo: shit. Since excreta flows out of the anus, the anus symbolises filth. Is that the case with gaand too? For a long time I believed so. However, if no equivalent of shit is a strong taboo how can the anus be a taboo in Hindi? On closer analysis I found that while *ass*, *asshole*, and *kiss my ass* are the dominant swearwords in English vocab, the dominant swearword in Hindi is gaand marna, which refers to anal sex. When someone tells you 'kiss my ass', she basically means kiss the part of my body from where faeces come out. But gaand marna clealy refers to the act of anal sex.

On closer investigation, more differences between ass-class of swearwords and gaand-class of gaalis propped up:

- The usage of gaand-class is mostly for **homoerotic jokes** and **expression of frustration** over a situation. When you say '*yaar professor ne gaand hi maar di*' (Dude, the professor has fucked me in the ass) you express a frustration by equating the problem to the pain involved in violation of anal modesty.
- Gaand marna is more gender specific than asshole or kiss-my-ass. In fact, it is only girls from whom I have received the kiss-my-ass cuss. A woman may very well use a gaand marna cuss, but then the cuss loses its literal impact.

The conclusion I reached at (albeit hastily) from above differences is that gaand marna is somehow related to homosexuality. Homosexuality is an age old phenomenon in Indian society. Many sculptures in Konark and Khajuraho showcase erotic love between same sex couples, even between humans and animals. There are many instances in ancient texts attesting to the preponderance of homosexuality in ancient India. The *Kamasutra* mentions male servants performing oral sex on their masters. In the *Rajatarangini* (chronicles of the kings of Kashmir), one king is described as an addict of both anal and vaginal sex. He had male favourites whom he caressed in public. The *Shilappadikaram* talks of a gift of thousand boy prostitutes (all dressed like women) made to Chera king Shenguttavan by a king from North India.[42]

From these instances one can conclude that homosexuality as a mass phenomenon has always been there in India, flourishing underground and at times proliferating into public life too. However, the general conservatism of Hindu society constantly tries to repress homosexual feelings. Gaand marna as a gaali is a projection into language of the repressed homosexuality of gay Indian men. As the society censors homosexuality, these sentiments get suppressed in the subconscious of a gay individual. But the subconscious mind cannot hold repressed sentiments for long; it needs an outlet. Hence the subconscious mind projects the repressed sentiments in disguised form – in the form of humorous gaalis enacting homoeroticism.

On closer analysis, I found even this explanation unsatisfactory. The percentage of homosexuals in any society is not significant. It is quite improbable that a gaali which started off as an expression of deviant sexual leanings could find widespread use and become a common gaali. This might be one of the minor reasons, but not the primary one. So what can be the root cause of homoeroticism?

I got my cue when watching the movie *3 idiots*. A typical ragging exercise is depicted in the movie. Freshers were left to the mercy of seniors in an engineering college hostels. While seniors made them do all kind of grotesque activities, these freshers were supposed to follow a ritual: pull down their pants and offer their gaand to seniors and say '*Shehenshah, tohfa hazir hai*' (My king, please accept this gift). Similar rituals are followed in various campuses all over India. Later in the movie when Rancho (Aamir Khan) sorts out problems faced by his friends (played by Madhavan and Sharman Joshi) they enact the same ritual and gift their gaand to Khan. By the act they basically acknowledged that Rancho is the boss. The act was an acceptance of Rancho as superior to them, very much the way these students were made to accept the senior as the boss. My conclusion was that gaand marna is somehow related to superiority-inferiority.

This cue led me into search of scholarly writings on this line. This search took me to the writings of Sudhir Kakar, and his shocking assertion linking gaand marna to one of the most prominent characteristics of Indian society: hierarchy.

Hierarchy and symbolism

Every human society has a hierarchical order of social relations. Yet no other society is as obsessed with hierarchy as our society. The caste system is a hierarchy of castes placed in society in order of their ritual purity. The Bhangi caste is called 'untouchable among untouchables' because members of other Dalit castes (who are themselves outcastes) do not touch the Bhangi fearing they may lose their caste purity! The patriarchal family is a hierarchy of male members of the family arranged in terms of their age. The patriarch may be too old and feeble, yet ideally the whole family has to follow his dictates. In the Mahabharata, Yudhisthir loses himself, his brothers, and a co-wife in a game of gambles. All others express their dissatisfaction but none challenges his act because he is at top of the hierarchy. He *owns* the family and its members.

The hierarchy in India is different from what it is in other societies. In a class-based society, for example, the lower class worker working for a capitalist is not servile to the capitalist. They have an **employer-employee relation** rather than a **master-slave relation**. In India, on the other hand, the boss is *sarkar* or *malik* (master). Indian bureaucracy is so hierarchal that sycophancy is protocol here, and any junior officer who behaves more professional than sycophant is considered arrogant. In traditional India, caste relations operated on the basis of Jajmani system. In the Jajmani system, a poor lower caste family (*kulin*) is attached for generations to a rich upper caste family (*jajman*). The *kulin* family serves the *jajman* family and the *jajman* family pays whatever it thinks fit. Hence what is called caste system was once slavery in disguise.

Hence hierarchy in India does not demonstrate status or economic standing in society, but hierarchical *relations*. It demonstrates **superiority** and **servitude**; right of the better-off over the worse-off. And hierarchy is important to Indians. The *saas-bahu* relation is so soured in Indian families because the *bahu* (daughter-in-law) is supposed to be subordinate and servile to her *saas* (mother-in-law). If the *bahu* succumbs, she literally becomes a servant in her in-laws' house. If she insubordinates and challenges *saas*' authority an Ekta Kapoor soap follows.

Further, hierarchy in India has to be publicly demonstrated by **symbolisms**. The *saas* has to be cruel on her bahu. From my personal observation, I have found that most *saas* are unnecessarily hard on their daughters-in-law. The junior bureaucrat has to bow extra low when wishing a senior officer. More the seniority of the senior, greater you have to bow. You have to stand with your hands crossed behind your back and talk in an artificial, servile tone. You have to laugh at his poor jokes and share his public opinion. Similarly, in public functions in traditional India participants had to sit as per their caste status. This protocol was public demonstration of caste hierarchy.

My contention is that the usage of gaalis is symbolic. Gaalis are linguistic expressions and words are symbols. Hierarchy has deeply seeped into us Indians, making us what sociologist Louis Dumont calls Homo Hierarchus. Homo Sapiens are members of the same species; Homo Hierarchus are members of the same hierarchy, albeit placed at different positions in the hierarchy. And this hierarchy has to be publicly demonstrated. To publicly demonstrate it, you have to show a person his *auqaat* (status/ social standing/ means of livelihood).

Chod, thok and fuck

I find symbolic expression of Indian obsession with hierarchy in many gaalis. For example, take gender hierarchy. There is no ambiguity in gender hierarchy in traditional Indian society. Men are superior to women. Over and out. That's why the word *chod* means man-fucking-woman. In English, you may say:

'Mr. X is fucking Ms. Y', or

'Ms. Y is fucking Mr. X', or

'Mr. X and Ms. Y are fucking'.

Fuck is quite a gender neutral word. Even screwing is. 'Ms. Y is screwing with Mr. X' is very much accurate usage of the word. But chod has gender-specific usage. You can say

'*Shri X ne Shrimati Y ko chod diya*' (Mr. X has fucked Ms. Y) or

'*Shri X Shrimati Y ko chod raha hai*' (Mr. X is fucking Ms. Y).

But you cannot say that Ms. Y is chod-ing Mr. X. This will be incorrect usage of the word chod. Chod word is symbolic of male superioriy over females in gender hierarchy. Sex is unilateral. Man indulges in sex for entertainment, at the cost of the woman who suffers the pain, the way a low caste underpaid worker slaves out for his *malik*. When one says '*X ne Y ko chod diya*', it implies a male dominance; that an Indian woman cannot fuck. She can only bc fucked. Hence you can say:

'*Shrimati Y Shri X se* ***chud*** *rahi hai*' (Ms. Y is getting fucked by Mr. X), or

'*Shrimati Y Shri X se* ***chudti*** *hai*' (Ms. Y gets fucked by Mr. X).

The other hindi swear for fuck, thok, is similar to chod in intent but much more abrasive. Its usage is also pretty gender-specific. 'Thok' literally means 'to drub' or to hammer or knock out.

Expression	Meaning
ठोंक देना (Thonk dena)	Drive in
ठोक ठाक (Thok thak)	Fiddle
ठोंकना (Thonkna)	Hammer
ठोंक देना	Knock out
ठोकना (Thokna)	Drub

Table 8. 1 Literal translations of 'Thok' gaali

'*Kya be, mein sun raha hun tu Y ko* ***thok*** *raha hai aaj kal?*'

(What man, I hear you are fucking Y these days).

'*Wo ladki to class ki har doosre ladke se* ***thukti*** *hai*'.

(That girl gets fucked by every second guy of the class).

So that the hierarchy is not challenged, social values censor that a virtuous woman should not enjoy sex but see it as a means to make children.

When used as a gaali, chod and thok mean mess with someone. When Ram has wronged Hari big time, you say '*Ram ne Hari ko chod diya*' (Ram has *chod*-ed Hari). You can also use *chod* to imply that Ram has double-crossed Hari. The obvious direct usage is:

'*mein tujhe chod dunga*', which means 'I will fuck you'.

Back to your gaand

When you swear at someone, depending on the context, you may want to convey the message that the receiver has lower *auqaat*. Hence there have to be gaalis that convey the message: 'stay in your *auqaat*' or 'I have superior *auqaat* than you'. Just like maderchod-behenchod gaalis challenge the receiver's *izzat* (see chapter 6), there must be gaalis that challenge the receiver's *auqaat*.

Sudhir kakar believes that homoerotic gaalis (such as gaand marna) are symbolic of hierarchy's importance to Indian psyche. In his words,

> The erect penis and the offer of the anus among human males, as among many other primates, are *symbolic* of an attempt to *establish a hierarchical order* in their relationships. The fantasy among Indian patients of anal assault by an authority

> figure reflects not so much the occult pleasure and guilt of anal eroticism as it does the (relatively unconflicted) acceptance of the dominance of "those in authority" and the wish to incorporate some of their power into oneself. The *high frequency* among *adolescent boys and young men in India* of swear-words with the general tenor, "*fuck you in the anus*", is another index of the common masculine preoccupation with *hierarchal status.*[43]

Kakar basically 'shifts the meaning of overt and fantasied references to anal sex away from discussions of sex and the body to a universal phenomenology of hierarchy.'[44] At first look, his contention may sound farfetched. Yet, I extol you to visualise your arse being violated by a person, say Gopal. Gopal possibly has had fantasies of anal sex and is enjoying. But you are suffering in silence (unless you are gay). You are bent over, your head low and your arse pointed high in the sky, in offering for Gopal's erect penis. This image is symbolic of your submission to Gopal.

During my grad days, a popular saying went like this:

'*Professors se panga na lo.*

Jab bhi toke pant khol do

Ewam gaand arpit karke jhuk jao'

(Don't challenge the professors.

Whenever they have a problem with you, remove your pants

And bend while presenting your arse in offering)

This saying is symbolic of submission to professors' authority. The high frequency of usage of gaand marna / gaand marwana is symbolic of Indian males' preoccupation with hierarchy. If I say '*mein tera gaand mar dunga*' (I will fuck you in the ass), I mean I will show my superiority over you: you are inferior to me.

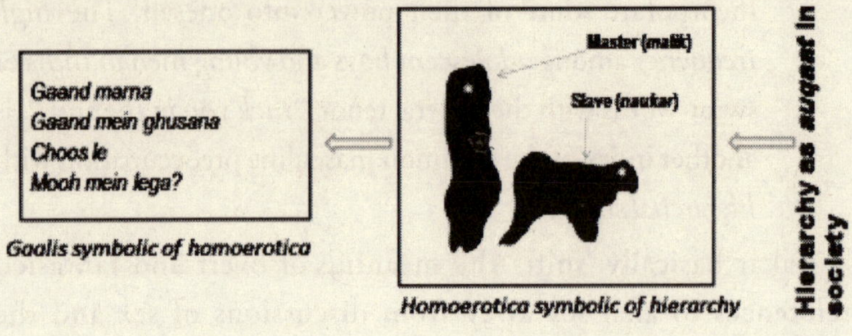

Figure 8. 1 Symbolism of social status in homoerotic gaalis

Mooh me lega?

On further analysis, I found the nexus between hierarchy and gaali quite deep. For example, it is difficult to find ethnic slurs used by people lower in caste hierarchy against those higher up. A friend tells me that at places where Dalits have captured political power, or are numerically superior the Brahmins are ridiculed[45] . Yet no stable slur against a higher caste has developed. This is because of the belief in caste hierarchy; the belief that some castes are ritually purer than other castes.

On a different note, references to oral sex in gaalis also point towards obsession with hierarchy. If someone tells you '*choos le*' (suck [my penis]), he implies that you are inferior to him. That's why he suggests you have his dick in your mouth. The references to oral sex in humour talk also shows auqaat. If Ram asks Hari to do him a big favour, say write a lengthy assignment, Hari can jocularly remark:

'*Ek shart pe… tujhe mera **mooh mein** lena hoga*'

(On one condition… you will have to take [my dick] in your mouth).

Hari basically means: if you expect me to do your work let me remind you that I have better (or equal) auqaat than that (by asking you to take my dick in your mouth).

What will excite a sociologist about gaalis is that while in the West taboos are used as swearwords per se, or to cause blasphemy, in India gaalis have a strong social under bearing. Though the swearwords refer to overt taboo references (incest, anal sex, genitals etc) they are directed at insulting not the individual but his *izzat* and his *auqaat*. This makes sense. People in Western societies are individualistic and status is individual status. But Indians have a collectivistic orientation[46] : we derive our self-identity from social groups we belong to which in turn derive their identity from their reputation (*izzat*) and status (*auqaat*) in society. Hence the covert symbolism of *izzat* and *auqaat* in major Hindi gaalis.

9

The Good about Bad Language

The utility of swearwords

A final puzzle about swearing is the crazy range of circumstances in which we do it. There is cathartic swearing, as when we hit our thumb with a hammer or knock over a glass of beer. There are imprecations, as when we suggest a label or offer advice to someone who has cut us off in traffic. There are vulgar terms for everyday things and activities, as when Bess Truman was asked to get the president to say fertilizer instead of manure and she replied, 'You have no idea how long it took me to get him to say manure.' There are figures of speech that put obscene words to other uses, such as the barnyard epithet for insincerity, the army acronym snafu, and the gynecological-flagellative term for uxorial dominance. And then there are the adjective-like expletives that salt the speech and split the words of soldiers, teenagers,

Australians, and others affecting a breezy speech style.

—Steven Pinker[47]

In certain trying circumstances, urgent circumstances, desperate circumstances, profanity furnishes a relief denied even to prayer

—Mark Twain

This happened to a friend. He was informed, at a very short notice, that a presentation he was supposed to make to the top bosses of his company had been preponed and he had just an hour's time. His immediate reaction was '*Saala*, an hour is too less'. On top of this, he was unable to find the excel sheet containing all the data. Someone had deleted the file from the computer.

'*Kya chutiye log hai yaar*' (What kind of *chutiya* my colleagues are) he exclaimed. By the time he got a back up file from a colleague the power went off and he cried out '*Bhenchod*'. At this point he got a call and he immediately yelled into his cell:

'Who is this *bhonsadi ke*'

It turned out his father had made the call.

This might have happened to you in the most unusual places. I once blurted out *lowda* in frustration when watching a cricket match at home (some Indian chap had got out). Luckily no one was around. But this made me wonder, why did I use gaali?

Any behaviour, any speech made is backed by a motive. There are two primary motives behind the usage of gaalis: psychological and social. In the case of my friend it was psychological. When he was swearing, he was swearing to himself. This is no perfect world, and we get frustrated or angry very often. This frustration is at unpleasant events and situations. It may be when you miss a bus or when you are made to write a software code all night or when you go to a cinema hall for entertainment and the movie turns out to be parallel cinema. In these situations you need a channel to vent out your frustration. Swearing serves to channelize the negative energy created by frustration and brings instant relief.

The capacity to respond to frustration is innate in us humans. When frustrated, infants de-stress themselves by crying[48] . My sister still uses the same mechanism to de-stress herself. If you have ever wondered why a grown up sister still cries when, say, you snatch the TV remote from her it is because a good cry gives instant relief to her frustrated mind. However, most cultures do not encourage crying among adults. Swearing comes up as a potent alternative for cathartic release of frustration.

This fact has been very amply demonstrated in the Hindi movie *Jab We Met*. In this movie, Shahid Kapoor encourages Kareena Kapoor to call up her boyfriend and swear at him. After using some gaalis, she seems to cheer up.

A gaali a day keeps the psychiatrist away

Visualise a situation in which you are having an altercation with another person. The best way to resolve the altercation is to fight it out. When a child I found it the best way to solve issues with kids smaller than me in size. But when I was bullied by a bigger *harami* I would run off and shout from a distance '*Ullu ka patha*'. Swearing at the bully helped me vent my aggression and brings me to an equilibrium state, without me getting into physical violence. On the other hand, there are those who have had a repressed childhood. They don't use gaalis because they have been severely reprimanded in childhood for swearing and thus they have internalised the belief that swearing is bad behaviour and only uncivilised people use gaalis. From my personal experience I have found them more unstable than myself in similar situations. Even if they are not, one strong channel of stress relief has been blocked to them.

Hence gaalis play a very important role in our lives. If all such altercations among men result in fights this world will be a much bloodier place to live in. As a verbal expression of aggression, gaalis help foster peace and order. In my opinion it is very important to expose children to soft gaalis. There are in-built mechanisms in society, such as peer groups and elder brothers to do so. But if your child does not get any of these, you better expose him to some of these.

Children also learn pretty fast what's the appropriate situation to use a gaali. When I was a kid, an elder cousin had used the word *dimba* in front of me. His friend had asked him a loan and he had said that he can only give a *dimba*. The word immediately resonated with me and I insistently asked the meaning of the word to him. He said it means egg in rural Oriya dialect, but warned me against using it anywhere. Later when an aunt asked me to pass on some water I told her I can only give her a *dimba*. Since I enjoyed the privileges of being an innocent kid, I was spared. But the cousin was thrashed. That day I realised never use *dimba* in front of family unless you seek revenge from an elder sibling. By the way, *dimba* is a muffasil Oriya word meaning balls (male reproductive glands).

The curious case of the monkey abuse

In the summer of 2008 the Indian cricket team was visiting Australia for a test series. These were the times when Indo-Australian on-field rivalry was at its peak. Pakistan was no longer opponent No.1. One of the strategies the Australian team used was sledging. They were aggressive and intentionally provoked the Indian players in order to distract them. In one such matches Australian player Andrew Symonds provoked Harbhajan Singh to such an extent that in fury he swore at Symonds. It is not clear what Bhajji told Symonds in the heat of the moment, but Symonds (and few other players) heard it as 'monkey'.

Monkey is a slur used by racists against Blacks. The Australian team accused Bhajji of racism. This became a big controversy and the matter ultimately went to ICC. Tendulkar, who is known for his integrity, was batting with Bhajji at the time and he vowed Bhajji had not given any monkey comment. Ultimately Harbhajan was found not guilty of racial abuse by the ICC judge. However, he was penalised for a smaller misconduct: of using abusive language on field.

As was subsequently speculated, Bhajji had actually yelled '*maa ki*' at Symonds (it might have been 'teri maa ki') and Australians misinterpreted it as monkey! It was reasoned that it is very unlikely for a brown Indian (the father of whose nation was thrown out of an all-white train in South Africa) to have colour feelings. A more scientific explanation of why the swearword was most probably *maa ki* is that Harbhajan was frustrated with the kind of sledging Australians were up to. At a time of extreme frustration, when one wants to dissipate the aggression he tends to swear in his mother tongue. And a Punjab-da-puttar would prefer mother-fucker over monkey. The motive behind the gaali was actually psychological – the gaali was reflexive and though directed at Symonds was not meant to insult his race.

Few months back, it came to news that the Aussies are trying to compile a list of gaalis in various Indian languages that could possibly be used to identify any non-racist swear from racist comments made by Indian audiences during India-Australia matches on Australian soil. But the dumb thing they did was to ask Indian team members to provide them with the list. How can a team of fifteen or sixteen possibly help them compile gaalis in myriad Indian languages! And if, say, a Gujarati screams *namaalo* (hermaphrodite in Gujarati) at Symonds in his accent, how are they going to process it in their list to differentiate it from negro?

Social motives

There are numerous reasons why one may use gaalis in a social setting. As one psychologist puts it, swearing 'is like using the horn on your car, which can be used to signify a number emotions'[49]. For example, rather than 'it's a very good movie', the expression 'it's a *bakchod* movie' expresses a stronger sentiment of satisfaction on watching a good movie. As has been demonstrated in an earlier chapter gaalis are most frequently used in interaction with friends, and demonstrate the emotions of affection and friendly disposition.

I recently met a close friend of grad days who had married just few days back. Although he never used gaalis in college, he very frequently used *maderchod*, *chutiya*, and fuck on the dinner table, much to the embarrassment of his wife and me. This is a trend I have seen in wannabes. They make frequent use of gaalis to look cool. They even swear in front of girls just to show off a machismo.

When coupled with right timing, swearing helps create humour in social settings. Party entertainers, stand up comedians and filmmakers very tactfully exploit this fact to entertain their audience. The producer-director Vishal Bharadwaj, for example, uses gaalis very frequently in his movies to create humour. His movie *Omkara* was one of the first mainstream Bollywood cinemas to use maa-behen gaalis bluntly. The movie *Kaminey* went a step further in that the movie name itself is a mild gaali. *Ishqiya*, on the other hand, introduced few local UP-ite lingos such as *Chootiyum Sulphate*[50] to the audience. To be frank, I have often resorted to PJish usages of gaali using a chick-lit writing style in this book even though this is meant to be a no-nonsense study of gaalis just because you chutiya readers would rather read this shit than a Ramachandra Guha or a Dalrymple and their readers take themselves too seriously to give this shit a shit.

I have also been told that gaalis are to sex talk what spices are to curry. Cussing gaalis is a good way to turn on your partner in bed. A modern day Caligula I interviewed confirms this belief. He says in bed women become receptive to swearwords like *raand* (another noun for the word *randi*, used when referring to the receiver in first person) and *bitch* which they would otherwise disapprove from a man's mouth. Further, a good sex talk heavily loaded with gaalis acts as an alternative to foreplay in bringing about a turn on.

Gender differences

There are gender differences on how frequently men and women use swearwords. Some western studies have revealed that men accounted for 67% of public swearing in 1986 while in 2006 the ratio had come down to 55%[51]. There being wide cross-cultural variations these figures do not throw any light on relative gender uses of gaali in India. From my personal interviews I found that the gaalis most frequently used by girls are of a mild nature: *kutti*, *kamini*, *raand* to name a few. Mothers frequently use colourful gaali like *chudail* and *dayan* to swear at unruly daughters.

The mother-daughter relationship in my household has always

been on rocks, and I have had the privilege to see at close quarters how mothers and daughters fight it out. One Oriya gaali that my mother quite frequently used for my sister was *chandi.* Interestingly, *Chandi* is a powerful form of Goddess Durga. As a woman of immense power and fury She is revered and feared by the faithful. Many Oriyas also consider her a symbol of female independence and gender equality. But somewhere down the line *chandi* became a derogatory word. This may be because of a duality of role models one finds in female Goddesses: Shakti, Kali, and Chandi on one hand, and Sita, Savitri, and Anasuya on the other[52] . The second group of Goddesses represent a model of female meekness, subordination and obedience. 'Good' women are supposed to conform to the Sita-Savitri model. When a mother curses her daughter as *chandi*, she basically implies that the daughter is not meek as women are supposed to be. At the same time, using a Goddess' name saves the mother from any guilt feeling at having cursed her daughter[53] .

But when it comes to severe gaalis, women are generally found not to use them. Few of the women I interviewed said that they have used *maa-behen* gaalis to swear at men. However, even *kutti* and *kamini* are not frequently used by women in their conversations. What can be the factors affecting this disparity of genders? One, men tend to get frustration-aggression syndrome more often. Evolutionarily men have been hunters and women gatherers. In other species too it is the males who fight it out – for females, for territory, and power. So men are more likely to get into situation involving aggressive energy. The need for men to dissipate this energy is more; hence greater usage of gaali.

A second reason is that our society severely discourages men from crying. Adults are not supposed to cry, but the expectation is more severe from men[54]. My sister still resorts to crying when I beat her up. But this kind of behaviour on my part would be considered unmanly. When I beat her up I end up with greater injuries, given the fact that she has long canine nails and is quite skilful in hurling heavy objects at me. But I never cry, just smirk at her basking in the glory of having beat her and the collateral pain.

And thirdly because a guy may use gaalis to assert his masculine identity in social interactions. A woman swearing is considered unfeminine and of a bad character. Just for the record, some men I interviewed get turned on by women who swear or smoke: both cuss and smoke have a horny aroma when coming out of a woman's mouth.

An explanation for the excessive censorship on women swearing is that women are not supposed to use them because women are responsible for observing religious rituals; hence they need to be pure. And purity includes purity of tongue. One scholar observes:

> ...these [swearwords] are forbidden to women. They are 'mardaana gaalis'. Many a woman writer in Hindi has been pilloried for daring to use a mardaana gaali... This is not surprising... since religious censorship placed the main onus of maintaining the sanctity and purity of everything, including language, on women.[55]

10

G-beep, F@#$ You

Law, censorship, and social change

I personally blame the movies and television for the loss of respect for swearing. Look at all those pathetic actors, swearing with no gusto, with no feeling at all at times. What might vulnerable youngsters pick up from that? They might get it into their heads that swearing needs no skills and is just a casual thing. Like sex. And swearing is much more important than sex. Animals can do sex too. They can do it even better than people, if you ask me. But swearing - that's where humans stand tall and walk alone. That's what the main and only difference is between men and beasts: we swear, they don't. The rest we share with animals: eating, sleeping, shagging, shitting and chilling out[56]

Sometime in my final years in school, Hindi movies became uncool in the 'dude circle'. The dudes animatedly discussed Titanic,

Star Wars and Terminator and laughed at how dumb Hindi movies were. As a wannabe follower of the dude circle it became impertinent for me to watch some English movies. How long could I have laughed at Hindi movies without knowing how cool English movies were! But there was a problem in this. My parents belong to the old school. Though few English channels were available on cable, they were tabooed in our home.

'They show bad films. Bad language, bad scenes' my father used to opine. His discomfort was evident when I watched TV with him and a stayfree secure advertisement popped up unawares. I could see in his eyes the desperation on not being able to stop the ad from screening.

But I guess times are changing. The other day I had visited my aunt's place. My much younger cousin offered to show me a new DVD he had bought. The movie was Jason Statham starrer *Crank 2: High Voltage*. As the name suggests it had a cranky storyline, every actor competing with every other actor in chanting the f-word. Almost every sentence had a cunt or a fuck. It seemed as if the dialogue writer had a cunt in his mouth or his mouth in a cunt when he wrote the dialogues. To top it Whites, Brazilians, and Chinese all were subjected to racial ridicule. When Statham could not understand a Chinese woman's speech he wondered if she was speaking cunt-onese (reference to Cantonese). In short it was a fucking crazy movie made by fucked up fuckers. And my cousin comfortably watched it while my aunt was hovering around all along.

When the movie started I loved the dialogues and the protagonist's crazy adventures. But after a point I got bored of all that. I mean, what the fuck was the fucking director thinking making a fucking movie full of fuck? His kindergarten teacher, it seems, had introduced him to only three words: fuck, fuck and fuck. A for fuck, B for fuck, C for cunt, and D for fuck. And if this movie has had a public release in America then how the fuck is fuck a swearword?

A swearword is a swearword because it is censored in public. Swearing and censorship are two sides of the same coin: a word cannot be taboo word as long as it is not censored, the way a fuck cannot be a fuck as long as there is not a dick and a hole. Alternatively, censorship is meaningless when there is no taboo word. And times are such that even kids bugged by mothers show the middle finger and shout 'fuck you mom'. Political leaders in the West use swearwords way too freely. Social change is a fact, but the pace of social change has increased manifold with the advent of visual media and the boundaries of the acceptable scene and obscene are fast blurring. On the face of it, how many of the traditional swearwords like fuck, suck, damn, hell (English), chutiya, gaandu, and saala (Hindi) can still be called swearwords?

> **JERK**
>
> The word had emerged in late nineteenth century as a verb meaning 'to masturbate'. But about three decades after its emergence it became a common noun meaning an obnoxious or offensive person.
>
> Hughes (2006), p.310-311.

Swearing & Social change

In order to better understand this fuck-isation of popular speech an exposition of a history of censorship is necessary. In pre-modern times human behaviour was regulated by informal but influential institutions. In the West it was the Church, in India the lobby of Brahminical ideology. The Church had imposed the most powerful form of censorship: religious censorship. As a result, blasphemous words constituted a majority of swearwords in the West then. References to sex were generally censored. However, every act of prohibition is met with defiance. Swearing is an act of defiance against censorship. Taboo leads to censorship and censorship leads to swearwords.

With the modernisation of tradition, informal institutions slowly lost their power. The onus of censorship passed on to formal institutions: law and government. A major breakthrough in this process was the codification of freedom of speech and expression as a fundamental right in democracies. With this codification traditional censorship lost much of its space to the obscene which now became the acceptable scene. Subsequently cultural diffusion facilitated introduction of new ideas of more modern societies in more traditional societies. Many taboos of yesteryears are no longer taboo. It is no longer taboo for a woman to take her husband's name; rather that act is old-fashioned.

Fashion is a second important reason for decay of censorship. By definition 'fashionable' refers to current social fashions. It is something new, not already in vogue in society. Frequent and casual swearing is new, not in vogue. As a result swearing becomes a style statement. Due to frequent usage, many foul words become fair words. Just as with skirts and cleavage displays, what is fashion today becomes retrograde tomorrow. Mild swearwords (like *harami*) lose their cuss character while severe swearwords like *maderchod* become mild. *Damn* and *O my God*, for example, are hardly swearwords these days. We Indians use them as punctuations to fill the gaps in our broken English, most of us quite unaware that they are blasphemous swearwords in Christianity faith.

Perhaps the most important reason for liberalisation of censorship is the advent of new ideas: ideas of egalitarianism. Previously there was a huge gulf between the cultured and the uncultured; the Brahmin and the Bhangi. This gulf in social position was justified by many myths, one of them being that the cultured are sophisticated, have good manners and fine speech. The lady was different from women. The gentleman was above common man. In order to distinguish itself from the subaltern, the pretentious high society cultivated puritan manners which came to characterise its members. Fine speech was one of them. Foul language was branded language of the uncultured and swearing was symbolic of uncivil behaviour. There was hence a stigma of status attached to swearing.

The play *My fair lady* was a provocative play of its time in British society in the sense that it portrayed a subaltern foul-mouthed woman who with right training becomes a lady. It conveyed the message that given the opportunity anyone can become part of high society. The message sounds absurd now because we have fast moved on to imbibe ideas of egalitarianism which breaks the whole myth of cultured and uncultured. Language has become more egalitarian. Formal language liberally borrows from parochial language. People of all class now freely swear without the fear of being stigmatised as uncultured.

Dynamics of swearing

Andrew Jones, a progressive theologian, contends that profane words can be broadly divided into three categories: *excommunicatory*, *explicit*, and *exclusionary*[57] . Excommunicatory refers to blasphemy: words that are considered offensive by religious bodies. Explicit refers to those words which refer to body parts and sexual and excremental functions of these. Whereas exclusionary words are 'racial, minorital, and misogynistic in nature, offensively used to label and marginalise'[58]. Based on this classification Adam Mellem, a scholar of postmodern theology, contends that the nature of swearwords has shifted from excommunicatory towards explicit towards exclusionary over time[59]. Although his analysis is based on Western societal history, it is relevant in Indian context too.

Excommunicatory words were strong taboos when religious bodies were powerful and religious censorship was severe. Violation of these taboos led to severe punishment, often *excommunication* from the community. However with increasing secularism excommunicatory swears have effectively become casual.

Explicit words were not swearwords in the ancient era. This is evidenced from the fact that there was no shame in display of body parts or bodily functions in ancient times. The explicit nature of images carved in various temples of ancient India, and the *devadasin* culture – devadasis had reasonable good social status – demonstrates that demonstration of body parts was liberal in that era. After all, as the cliché goes, kamasutra was written in India. As the saying goes sage Vatsyayan, a scholar of repute, had stayed in brothels with his research assistants and observed (it is not clear which research method he used: participant observation or non-participant observation; since he was funded by rich landlords, he certainly had the means to participate) various arts of love making practised therein before writing this book.

Explicit terms became taboo with the advent of what Mellem refers to as 'shame standard' in society. Shame standard started with the upper stratum and moved downwards. New conventions of social standards developed that considered talk of body parts involved in sexual functions vulgar. It was then that explicit words became swearwords. An alternative explanation, found mostly in rightwing writings, is that shame standard was adopted by medieval India from its Islamic gentry. Shame of bodily parts was strongly embedded in Turkish and Persian customs even at the time when Turks and Afghans came to India[60]. However this explanation being tainted with ideology needs to be taken with a pinch of salt.

Nature of explicit swearwords takes a U-turn in contemporary times. Bodily display and sexual functions are still censored, but the boundary is fast shifting: owing mostly to the freedom of expression and power of mass media, especially motion pictures. As a result, words like dick and fuck are fast losing their severity. One can mark the increase in liberal use of fuck from a casual observation of English movies in the last two decades.

This brings us to the third category, exclusionary words. While excommunicatory swearwords have turned sterile and explicit words are fast turning sterile, exclusionary words are becoming more profane by the day. The preponderance of exclusionary swearwords is but evident from the enhanced rate of racial contact resulting from migration in last few centuries, more so in last few decades. Racial and ethnic contact is followed by tendencies of discrimination and social exclusion of minority ethnic groups. Ethnic slurs such as nigger and mleccha are acts of subordination by the majority ethnicity over the minority. When minority communities take exception to these slurs, it is an act of censorship.

The censorship of ethnic abuse is on a rise. This is both because of formal laws prohibiting discrimination and opposition by civil society. The word nigger, for example, has been in the middle of lot of controversy of late. Many celebrities, singers, and stand-up comedians have been severely punished for using the N-word in public, whatever the intention of using the word may be. In India, discrimination against the lower castes and tribes was embedded in traditional society. Casteist slurs were not proscribed but rather prescribed. The social reform movements of early nineteenth century marked the beginning of the end. This was followed by backward class movements and post-independence political dynamics. Today backward caste associations and their political formations are influential. These bodies censor caste-based discrimination and by extension casteist slurs. The press, literati and human rights groups also play significant role in censorship of caste-based slurs, and those which target minority groups in general. The law also censors ethnic slurs: protection against discrimination is a fundamental right while specific acts have been formulated for prevention of discrimination against SC/ST communities.

Another sub-category of exclusionary words are words that are misogynistic or sexist in nature. Words such as *chut* and *maal* come in this category. Feminist scholars and activists are primarily identified with censorship of these words, although the Supreme Court and law enforcement agencies also play a critical role in censorship of sexism.

An interesting observation in the dynamics of swearing is that it is reactive; profanity is proportional to censorship. When a society moves from being religious to being secular, excommunicatory words become less profane. When a majoritarian society becomes more inclusive and democratic, exclusionary words become more profane. The deal with explicit words is more complicated: their degree of profanity depends on definition of obscenity and shame standards in current society. Still, a pattern can be observed in dynamics of explicit swearwords: they are becoming increasingly mild.

Censorship today

Censorship in contemporary India derives from two sources: formal (law and Censor Board) and informal (moral police, religious institutions etc) institutions and agencies. Unlike in the West, informal institutions still wield influence among Indian masses. One may wonder why.

Religious censorship is always the most powerful censorship among informal sources. While in the West censorship was imposed by the Church, there was no such institution in India. Rather the most apparent institutionalised form of religion was caste. The Church lost most of its political power post-Renaissance. However, upper castes of India retained much of their traditional power till mid-20th century, Indian society then still being semi-feudalistic. Owing to various reasons[61] caste hierarchy started degenerating. But the power of castes did not degenerate completely. Castes metamorphosed into caste associations: pressure groups influencing government's decision making by participation in politics.

Unlike castes caste associations are secular bodies formed for the singular objective of furthering interests of caste members. Caste system today is a bunch of caste groups competing for political power. Hence castes have become more or less secular in character. So has religious censorship vanished? May be not. New right wing organisations catering to Hindu, Muslim, Sikh, and Christian clientele took up the responsibility of religious censorship. These associations are basically pressure groups with huge influence in national and regional politics, and they derive their power from participation in politics. These organisations have censored what in their perception distorts the basic tenet of religion, culture, social values and morals.

However, no major objection to use of gaali has been raised by the moral brigade (gaali here does not include exclusionary terms, whose censorship has already been discussed). At present the only organised sources of censorship of gaalis are law and its organs: the courts and Censor Board.

Apna Haath Jagannath

In the movie Kaminey, one scene showed a wall sketch (the type you find in most college walls) inside a latrine. The sketch depicted a nude woman with *Apna Haath Jagannath* written over it. This scene was passed by censor board but post-release there were severe objections to the use of Lord Jagannath's name alongside a nude woman's sketch inside a latrine. The priests of Puri's Jagannath temple criticised the depiction and soon a furore rose in many parts of Orissa against the movie.

Apna Haath Jagannath literally means 'your own hand is God' and is used in the sense that hard work is divine. However an alternative meaning is masturbation. If you don't get lucky, use your hand: anytime, anywhere. The agitators had taken exception to this meaning and the nude woman's sketch. They found both of these blasphemous.

This is one of many instances of censorship by informal organisations. Organisations such as the Shiv Sena and Maharashtra Navnirman Sena have many a times stopped screening of movies objecting depiction of varied issues like communal riots, lesbian relations, and calling Mumbai Bombay.

Law on gaalis

Article 19 (1)(a) of the constitution guarantees every citizen a right to freedom of speech and expression. However, this right is subject to conditions mentioned in clause (2) of article 19. The state can make laws to impose reasonable restrictions on freedom to speech and expression 'in the interests of the sovereignty and integrity of India, the security of the State, friendly relations with foreign States, public order, decency or morality, or in relation to contempt of court, defamation or incitement to an offence.' Restrictions on usage of expletives in speech and expression can be on counts of 'decency' and 'morality'. It must also be appreciated that decency and morality widely differ in definition across societies and within a society across time periods. The constitution makers had realised that a definite, objective definition is not possible; hence they had left the matter to interpretation of lawmakers and the apex court from time to time by using the words 'reasonable restrictions', 'decency', and 'morality'.

Based on the spirit of reasonable restrictions on freedom of speech and expression, the Cinematograph Act of 1952 was passed and Censor Board was established vide this Act to test and rate motion pictures. The Censor Board is today the most influential censoring authority in the country. One may wonder why this focus on motion pictures. No official body to censor print media or theatre exists. This may be because of the much more influential nature of cinema on the masses. While the print media only reaches out to the literate, cinemas have much wider access. In K. A. Abbas case[62] , Chief Justice Hidayatullah had upheld film censorship arguing that the impact of motion pictures is *different* from that of other forms of art and expression:

> *The instant appeal of the motion picture, its versatility, realism (often surrealism), and its coordination of the visual and aural*

senses...The art of the cameraman, with trick photography, vistavision and three-dimensional representation thrown in, has made the cinema picture more true to life than even the theatre or indeed any other form of representative art. The motion picture is able to stir up emotions more deeply than any other form of art. Its effect particularly on children and adolescents is very great since their immaturity makes them more willingly suspend their disbelief than mature men and women. They also remember the action in the picture and try to emulate or imitate what they have seen....A person reading a book or other writing or hearing a speech or viewing a painting or sculpture is not so deeply stirred as by seeing a motion picture

The Censor Board rates movies and certifies them for public access. 'U' certificate is given to a film suitable for unrestricted public exhibition while 'UA' rating is given to films that are suitable for public exhibition subject to adult supervision of children. 'A' rating is given to movies suitable for unrestricted adult exhibition. In certifying films the Censor Board is provided with guiding principles in section 5-B of the Cinematograph Act. Section 5-B is but a reflection of reasonable restrictions placed on freedom of speech and expression in Art.19(2) of the constitution. Hence these guidelines are also broad-based and subjective. The Supreme Court has acknowledged the fact in Bobby Art International case[63] .

This case dealt with the issue of censorship of the movie 'Bandit Queen'. The movie was shot in Chambal valley and narrated the true story of dacoit Phoolan Devi. As a girl, Phoolan Devi was forced to marry a man much older to her in age. She was beaten up and raped by him. Subsequently she was harassed, both sexually and otherwise, by upper caste boys of her village, the village panchayat, police, and outlaws. Later she kills the dacoit leader Babu Gujjar and becomes a dacoit. This film was a first in Indian cinema in the sense that lot of violence and nudity was displayed in the film. The movie also uses lots of expletives.

The censor board had recommended that the movie be given A certificate subject to certain cuts and modifications. Not happy with the censoring, the producers appealed against it in the appellate tribunal. Ultimately the matter went up to Supreme Court which upheld the appellant's arguments. The Supreme Court had then observed that the guiding principles laid down in section 5-B of Cinematograph Act are broad standards and should not be read as one would read a statute. The Supreme Court further stated that the authorities concerned with film certification should be responsive to the values and standards of society as well as take note of social change. The authorities should ensure that artistic expression and creative freedom are not unduly curbed. A film must be judged in its entirety from the point of view of its overall impact; and 'in the light of the period depicted and the contemporary standards of the people to whom it relates, but it must not deprave the morality of the audience.' This judgment was a landmark in the sense that it widened the scope for Censor Board to interpret what constitutes vulgarity, obscenity and depravity.

The Censor Board has been making increasingly liberal interpretations of vulgarity and obscenity in recent times. This is evidenced from the rise in use of swearwords in Hindi cinema. There was a time when films never went beyond 'Kutte, kaminey…' which in fact got stereotyped with a furious Dharmendra. There were also the occasional use of randi and kutti by bold directors of the time.

The movie that can be tagged as a milestone in screen cussing is *Monsoon Wedding*. Made by Mira Nair in 2001, it was actually an international production; not from Bollywood factory. Yet the movie was well received by Indian audience and signed the relaxation of swearword censorship. However, the real credit for this trend goes to a new breed of filmmakers led by likes of Vishal Bharadwaj and Anurag Kashyap. Vishal Bharadwaj has consistently used expletives in his films (save but the two children's films *Makdee* and *Blue Umbrella*) and to good effect. In *Omkara* he had made liberal use of chutiya and maa-behen gaalis in a West UP-ite rendition of Othello. Next he made a movie which he named *Kaminey*. In *Ishqiya*, which he produced and scripted, he went a step further and made use of intelligent euphemisms to add spice to dialogues.

Kashyap makes liberal use of gaalis in his masterpiece *Gulaal* and his other movie *Dev D*. Expletives are frequently used in *Dev D*, and both by male and female actors. Kashyap's team had also made an X-rated version of *Dev D*'s hit song 'Tera Emotional Atyaachar…' The X-rated version was creative and full of Punjabi expletives; it was an instant hit in YouTube. *Gulaal* is more of a poem than a movie, a poem in Rajasthani Hindi splattered with expletives.

Certain words, such as *saala*, have pretty much ceased to be a swearword in Bollywood thanks to songs like '*Eh saala, abhi abhi…*' (movie Rang De Basanti) and '*Pappu can't dance saala…*' (movie Jaane Tu Ya Jaane Na), the pappu song being a favourite number among school children. Recently I had attended a school function in which children danced to this number.

Yet a fact that needs to be appreciated is that swearwords when not used in the right context may sound embarrassing and distasteful. A directorial venture of Priyadarshan released in 2010, *Khatta Meetha*, is a case in point. In this movie a character uses the word 'gaand marna'. The dialogue delivery is abrupt, loud, and forceful. Gaalis in dialogues end up as orphans if not properly integrated with the scene and same happened with this scene. Many other gaalis used in the movie meet similar end because they have thoughtlessly been inserted without integrating them to the context.

TV channels such as Channel V and M-TV, both catering to a teen audience host reality shows in which most actors are foul mouthed. Even though expletives are beeped, the audience can guess which word an actor mouths. Certain show trailers also feature expressions like 'f@^k' written in large fonts. *MTV Roadies, GPL,* and *Splitzvilla* are some reality shows aired on these channels that constantly test the boundaries of acceptable language and profanity. The serial name *GPL* is actually an acronym for *Gaand pe Laat* (Kick on the ass). In this show two men or women compete for the attention of one partner. The show gets real dirty when two ladies fight it out for a guy. Cat fights in *GPL* are heavily laden with beeped-out expletives, and the editors ensure that the audience recognize which expletive is spoken by the participants beneath a beep. Ultimately the guy selects one of the girls and the other gets a *gaand pe laat. MTV Roadies* was once The Craze. It's the cult show of my late teenage, and of the many fads it inspired one was girls swearing. While a foul-mouthed girl is generally a turn-on, this show overturned the stigma attached with young women swearing.

The show *Emotional Atyaachar*, aired in UTV Bindaas, is the latest craze among the fourteen year olds. In this show a guy or a girl does a loyalty test on his (her) partner. If a girl wants to know how loyal her boyfriend is to her, she takes the help of a team of sleuths. This team creates a realistic plot and implants a hot babe in her boyfriend's life. Within few days the poor boyfriend gets cosy with this girl thinking he is getting lucky, and all this is recorded by spy cameras for the audience's entertainment. Finally when the girl confronts this guy, expletives flow like fire crackers. The show is mostly a drag, and swearing is the part audience love the most. What if a large part of the furious girlfriend's lambast is beeped and undecipherable. I have seen fourteen year old kids fervently watch the show in front of parents. This is a show I would not have dared watch in my house when I was fourteen. Just a decade's time has brought about this wide drift in parental attitudes. Or may be parental attitude has not changed; it is the dilution of swearwords which makes programmes such as *Emotional Atyaachar* acceptable at home.

Yet when compared with Hollywood, freedom of expression of expletives is still strongly regulated in Bollywood. Censor Board reprimands moviemakers with cuts when it feels that the use of expletives is unnecessary in the context of the scene or the story. Likes of Kashyap and Bharadwaj could tide through the Censor Board because they try to make realistic portrays in their movies. *Gulaal* would lose much of its impact if expletives as used in colloquial dialects of Rajasthan are removed from dialogues. Same goes with *Omkara*. In Dev D, Abhay Deol's character uses lots of gaalis. This helps bring out the character, and deletion of gaalis would rob the movie of proper character building. When Chanda explains that she is a Commercial Sex Worker because it has become unfashionable to call sex workers *randi*, it brings out a facet of her personality.

It is long time for cranky movies such as *Crank* getting through Indian Censor Board. Hollywood boasts of some memorable movies in which every second dialogue starts with a fuck. The cult movie *Pulp fiction* boasts of 265 fuck counts while an earlier movie by the same director *Reservoir Dogs* had a total of 269 fuck counts. Dialogues of *Lock, Stock and Two Smoking Barrels*, a movie by Guy Ritchie, were replete with swearwords and not just fuck, every damn swearword in English vocabulary. However given the pace with which expletives are losing their profanity and censorship is surrendering ground, the day when an Indian avatar of Crank gets aired at a multiplex in your neighbourhood is not far.

[illegible]

Vol 2

11

Curse Control

The dummy's guide on how to manage public swearing

Profanity is the common crutch of the conversational cripple

—David Keuck

Profanity is the attempt of a lazy and feeble mind to express itself forcefully

I'll tell you this: people don't really treat swearing seriously anymore. Take the most important rule: use F-words and other swear-words sparingly, otherwise they lose their sparkle. What the hell happened to this rule? Why is it that we hear some politicians and ordinary folk say f..k this and f..k that, all over the bloody place, all the bloody time? This indiscriminate swearing cheapens the whole thing and even such gems as the F-word and the C-word start to sound casual, almost normal like.[64]

There is a conceptual difference between a foodie and an obese. The difference is that of normality and abnormality. Anything in excess is harmful and swearing is no exception. All through this book I have romanticised the idea of swearing because swearing is a part of our life. Gaalis are colourful projections of who we are, what we are. Yet swearing can become dysfunctional if used too frequently in language.

We shall begin this chapter with the question: can swearing develop into an addiction? Addiction is the abnormal dependence on something psychologically or physically. Swearing can only lead to psychological dependence. And as you must be aware, swearing does develop into a habit in some people. There are people who swear compulsively, in almost every sentence. And they continue doing so even when advised by others not to do so in certain places. Yes, swearing can turn into an addiction. Of course, the clinical definition of addiction is much different and a habit of swearing is not regarded as addiction, unless swearing is a behavioural manifestation of a Generalised Anxiety Disorder (GAD) or Obsessive Compulsive Disorder (OCD).

Now, are you an addict? In my opinion there is a good chance you are if you show any or many of the following symptoms:

- Language for you is bad language. Swearwords are almost all the vocabulary you got.
- You cannot differentiate between situations in which cuss words can be used liberally and formal situations.
- Even if you can, you still end up swearing in public places.
- You don't swear at the wrong place but you are conscious about it; or have to consciously make an effort not to swear.

- You swear at the wrong place and then realise that you have used a swearword.
- You don't swear frequently, but you can't help but swearing when a **trigger situation** emerges, for example, when you have to stand in a queue or when it is too hot or cold.

Swearing as a habit has many disadvantages. When swearing is used occasionally, it has an 'impact value'. Frequent swearing robs a swearword of its impact. People don't take a man with a foul mouth seriously. Nor is it pleasant to converse with an acquaintance (who is not a close friend) who swears habitually. Swearing habit can be highly damaging for the addict in his office. If you utter as much as a simple 'maderchod!' exclamation in front of colleagues and superiors, they may judge you as uncultured and one without a proper upbringing.

Swearing at the wrong place at the wrong time can lead to unwanted violence against you. In Malay language, 'Terima Kashi' (pronounced teri-ma-ka-C) means thank you. You won't get into any problem for screaming *Teri Maa Ki* in Malaysia. But in India *Teri Maa Ki* has various meanings and conveys numerous emotions. It is not the meaning that you intend that matters but the interpretation made by the listener that does. Say a friend introduces you to his girlfriend and you blurt out: 'Dude your girl is a *patakchod maal*'. You say that as a compliment, but your friend takes it as he *interprets* what you say. If he makes the wrong interpretation you get a hard kick in the arse. Say you find yourself in the midst of a communal flare up. Some Hindu fanatics are raping a Christian nun alleged to have converted tribal youths. Just the gore of the scene makes you exclaim '*vhaanchod*'. It is just an exclamation and not directed at these fanatics but what if they take the word offensively. For all you know, they may leave the nun for the time being and come get your arse. These fanatics, I am told, are sex starved desperados who join riots just to get a hole.

Three steps to degalification

The difference between addiction (bad habit) and clinical addiction is that the individual can still manage an addiction himself whereas he needs specialists to help him out from a clinical addiction. Gaali addiction is a bad habit, and as with other habits it is tough to get rid of, but if the individual has the willpower he can exercise control over the habit.

Degalification is the process of gaali management; of being able to get rid of habitual swearing. In the next few pages I will be presenting a simple user guide to help you degalify and improve your personality. There are three basic steps I want you to follow and see the results for yourself. These three steps are:

1. Contemplation
2. Action, and
3. Relapse management

1. Contemplation

To get rid of a bad habit first you need to recognise that you have a habit and it's bad. Many people with a swearing addiction stay in a state of denial. It is only when something really embarrassing happens they realise they need to act. Trust me; the best time to start working on eliminating this habit is now. Longer you take stronger the habit becomes and tougher it is to degalify.

Once you have consciously articulated your intention to get rid of swearing addiction, the next step is to understand why it has developed into a habit: *root cause analysis.* When you repeat a behavioural pattern too frequently the behaviour tends to become involuntary. One does not have to consciously make an effort to elicit that behaviour. First you swear. Then it becomes frequent. Then a habit.

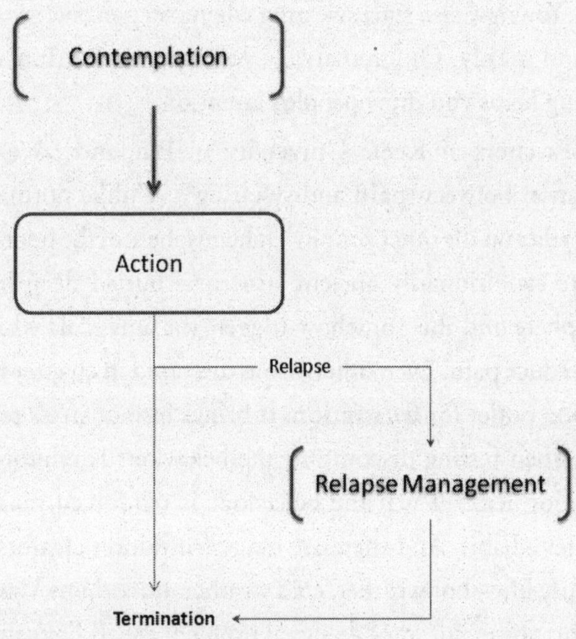

Figure 11.1 Three step process for degalification

Frequent swearing can develop due to a variety of reasons. You need to recognise the reason why you started swearing frequently. Does your father swear? Many a times when **parents swear** in front of a child, the child vicariously learns to swear. He has never learnt to exercise self-control over swearing. It also becomes tough for him to *differentiate* situations where swearwords are not appropriate. Bad language is the only language you know.

Peer groups are an important source of many bad habits. Swearing is, in fact, an identifier for peer groups. In college the language in which one talks to members of his group is different from the way he talks to others. Some groups use more swearwords than other groups, and swearing becomes an identifier of the group. SO if you become part of the group you start swearing to identify with the group. You may also start swearing when you perceive swearing to be **cool** and **manly**. Or alternatively you are an **attention seeker** and swearing helps you draw people's attention.

Researchers at Keele University in England have found an association between **pain** and swearing[65] . Unlike normal language which relies on the outer zone in left hemisphere of the brain, expletives activate evolutionarily ancient structures buried deep inside right hemisphere and this somehow triggers the amygdala which in turn helps reduce pain. Even otherwise as discussed in chapter 8, swearing is a good outlet for **frustration**. It brings instant stress relief. If you swear when feeling discomfort, the behaviour is reinforced by the frustration leak. When the behaviour is reinforced many times it becomes a habit. And there are many frustration creators in today's fast, busy life – hot weather, cold weather, missed bus, dysfunctional elevator, power cut, mobile signal problem etc. Today's man is more prone to frustrations, hence more in need of swearwords. Yet this may develop into a habit.

It also helps to search for a **trigger**. Swearing may develop into a habit due to what is called *Classical Conditioning* in psychology jargon. In classical conditioning, if one behavioural pattern (here swearing) is performed after another (the trigger) many times, an association between the two develops. As a result, whenever you sense the trigger you swear. The trigger can be just anything; it can be the weather (humidity, heat etc), adrenaline rush, anger, nervous feeling, or an animal in the vicinity.

Lack of a **good vocabulary** can also lead to compulsive swearing. The most distinct feature about swearing in any language is that a swearword can be used to convey myriad feelings. What may need a bunch of good words to convey is easily conveyed by using gaalis. Swearwords are like words written in **bold** or *italics*. They stand out and convey emphasis. If you are too lazy in conversing, in all probability you won't make an effort to use the right words nor will you use higher pitch to emphasise where needed. Swearwords turn out to be good substitute for inability to express in so many words.

After you (a) realise that you have a bad habit, (b) decide to get rid of it, and (c) have made a root cause analysis, you are ready to start the degalification process.

2. Action

The key to this stage is willpower. You got to be diligent and put the extra effort to degalify yourself. As for the action you need to take, there is no one recipe. Rather you need to follow a multiplicity of strategies:

a. **Avoid nonchalant swearing**

   When you got a bad habit you use it way too often. So start by making an effort to remove swearing from casual conversation itself. If you are conscious about it, this helps. This did help my friend Meepak Dallik; the man who used to swear the way he has to breathe had to degalify himself when he got to know that his wife was pregnant. And it was an emergency, he was clear that he could not swear in front of his kid.

   To degalify himself he would consciously think before he

spoke. In just a month's time he had some control over his swearing. Now this can be a tough task for some, especially those who speak fast and without giving much thought. But then, who said it is easy?

b. **Improve vocabulary**

Some people curse because they are perpetually in a bad mood, or get angry too soon. But most swear just to express various emotions – happiness, frustration, melancholy etc. If you want to learn a better way to express yourself, you need to know more words. Learn some common words that would help you express your emotions in a more polite way. This is also your chance to be a better communicator.

c. **Usc cuphemisms**

Euphemism is an inoffensive and indirect substitute for an offensive word. For example, if instead of *chutiya* you say *Kenya* it's a euphemism. For *maal* use the word *daal.* While you fulfil your urge to swear it does not insult people near you. At the same time, your frequency of using chutiya decreases. This works wonders. A euphemism I frequently used during my days of degalification was *Ashok Leyland.* While also being the name of a popular brand of heavy vehicles manufacturer, Ashok Leyland actually stands for *Ashok le land* (Ashok suck a dick) or *Ashok ka le land* (have Ashok's dick [in your mouth]). When I call a chap named Shyam as 'Shyam Leyland' I actually mean 'Shyam suck a dick'.

During my undergrad days we people were given a hard time by heartless professors at laboratories of electrical technology department. These professors were infamous across the institute for the inhuman ways in which they used to bully students and ask for experiment repeats. Frustrated that I was, I always feared that I may end up abusing a professor or get so angry that I would lose my mind. My lab partner gave a way out; he asked me to say MOFO every time I felt like swearing. Mofo stands for Mother Fucker, and worked quite well all through my four years in electrical technology department. The professors once did not doubt that the word meant what they were; they considered it gibberish.

d. Use second language

Most of us Indians are bilingual, some trilingual. You must have noted that one tends to swear most in the language he is most comfortable with. Usually one is prone to swear most in the mother tongue. A good way to avoid swearing is to make the maximum talking in a second language: Hindi or English. Since many of us are not that fluent in the second language, we think in our mother tongue, then translate it into the second language and then speak. This gives enough time to a person to censor out swearwords from his speech.

e. Take help

Be articulate about your intention to stop swearing. Tell your girl friend, your peers, pals, and family. Ask them to interfere and point out if you use swearwords when talking. Also avoid conversing with pals who use too much swearwords for the period you act on your degalification. Research has demonstrated that social swearing is inhibited by the lack of appreciative audience or company of non-swearers[66].

f. Learn to discriminate

Of the problems of swearing addiction, the gravest is the problem of swearing at the wrong places: your office, formal dinner, business meetings to name a few. This may happen when swearing is so subconsciously rooted that it becomes involuntary. Alternatively this may happen when you cannot differentiate between contexts. If this is the reason you swear a lot draw a list of places and people where/ with whom you cannot use swearwords. This will help you recognise situations where you need to be extra careful.

g. **Anger management**

Gaalis have many colours, but they are most lethal when used in black & white. It is anger which strips gaalis and presents them in their literal meaning. *Maderchod* means motherfucker only when shot with anger. And it is when maderchod is said with anger that it offends the receiver. If you frequently lose your cool and get down to gaali mode, you need to do some anger management. Do meditation or yoga. Practice some self-control and self-talk techniques those manuals on anger management suggest. It will help.

I would specifically recommend the Vipassana technique of meditation for effective degalification. The philosophy of Vipassana is that an individual is generally a *bhogi* (participant) which causes mental disturbances. As a *bhogi* you try to interpret a situation or a message relative to yourself. When you get angry or frustrated it is because you consider yourself a participant in the situation/ conversation. You feel insulted or enraged at a comment because you are participating in the conversation. Vipassana helps you learn how to become a *drishta* (observer). While a *bhogi* is an actor, a *drishta* is a viewer. The *drishta* observes and analyses the external environment (situations and conversations) and the inner self (why am I feeling insulted? Why am I feeling hurt?) to arrive at conclusions. Being a value neutral analyst, the *drishta* is calm and composed.

h. Set realistic goals

Goal setting makes your degalification exercise systematic. Keep a count of the number of times you use swearwords in a day and vow to improve on it the next day. Check your weekly improvement and compare with past history. But mind you, keep realistic targets. If you keep a target you cannot meet and then you miss the target you will be demotivated. Also remember that the rate of decrease of swearword usage will be like a logarithmic curve: as the number of times you use swearword decreases the rate of decrease decreases too. It is not necessary to go down to zero point. After all cursing is not bad, over-cursing is.

When setting goals remember the SMART formula psychologists recommend:

SMART Goals = Specific
Measurable
Action-oriented
Realistic
Time-bound

a. Aversion

Classical conditioning happens when one event or behaviour is linked to another event or behaviour. You ring a bell and then feed a dog repeatedly. On seeing food the dog salivates.

After some repetitions ring the bell but don't feed it. Even then the dog salivates. This is because bell ring and food have got connected in the dog's brain.

Aversion works on similar lines. Every time you swear, think about something unpleasant: traumatic tortures you got from an authoritarian father in childhood, your ex-girlfriend cosy with her new beau, or just gory images. These images are not pleasant and you would not like to have them. When event-1 (swearing) gets connected to event-2 (aversive memory) you tend to avoid event-1 to avoid event-2.

j. **Rewards and punishment**

Reward increases the frequency of behaviour while punishment decreases the frequency of the behaviour. So you need to reward yourself for increasing the frequency of not swearing and punish yourself for decreasing the behaviour of not swearing. When you manage to meet your targets reward yourself with some good food. If you relapse or cannot meet your targets, treat the friends who have been helping you degalify. Don't forget to invite me. ☺

3. Relapse management

Now that you are in control of your tongue how does it feel? Good, I am sure. You use social swearing only at the right place, at the right time. When you use it the words have more impact than what previously was the case. At the same time you see a marked improvement in the way people perceive you.

But this is not end of the story. There is always the risk of relapse into habitual swearing. It is also possible that you don't realise when you have relapsed. If you cannot detect a relapse, you will have to start the process all over again with contemplation over your habit. Hence it is necessary for you to keep taking feedback. Ask close friends to keep a tab of your use of cuss words. Or take a count once in a while. If you find a drastic increase in swearword usage over the date of termination you need to do another short goal setting exercise.

A problem with relapse is *self-fulfulling prophecy*. If X relapses once he thinks he can never get rid of his swearing habit. This becomes a prophecy. And because he thinks he can never get rid of the habit, his willpower to manage relapses decreases. When his willpower decreases relapses become more freaquent thus proving his prophecy: he can never get rid of his swearing habit. Hence it is very important for you to understand that with perseverance you *will* cope swearing addiction. Don't be discouraged by few lapses. To keep your motivation level high do some self-talk.

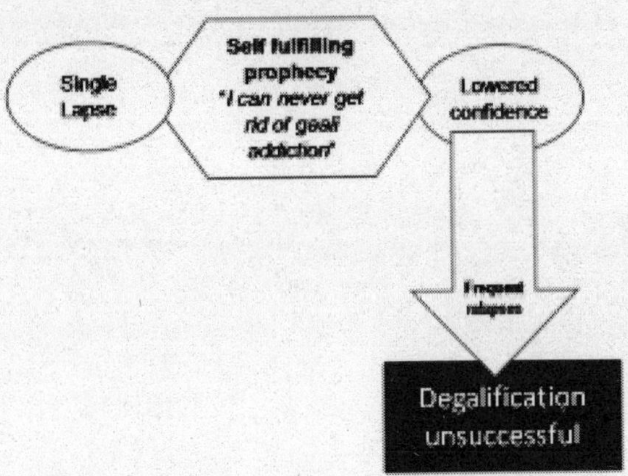

Figure11.2 Self fulfilling prophecy in failure of degalification

In my personal opinion good language and bad language are just labels given by the capitalist class to make us believe in their fake superiority. Good language is part of a greater nexus of cultured and refined tastes, a myth created by capitalists to show that they deserve being rich because they are sophisticated. Swearing is a characteristic of 'gutter talk' and shows how crude and unsophisticated the proletariat are. Hence the distinction between street slang and office communication. Hence the word foul in foul language. This inequality is symbolic of social inequality.

But then capitalism is the most viable option available to democracies. They set the rules, you follow them. If the rule is no maderchod behenchod in elite circles, you got to let go of these so as to be taken seriously by the dominant class. You got to let go of expletives and express your displeasure or pleasure in 'refined' language. That's why you need to be in control of your tongue. If that's a problem, high time you started degalifying yourself.

12

Expletive Effettivo

The dummy's guide to swearing across India

There are worse words than cuss words, there are words that hurt

—Tillie Olsen

The art of swearing has high utilitarian potential in myriad arenas. Alas, few know of this potential and even fewer can apply this to real life advantage. If you are a business executive or an entrepreneur constantly in the lookout of *jugaad* (networking), right swearing at right places helps tremendously in forming quick social links. Same applies for a traveller with an interest in interacting with peoples from different cultures. For a trainer, swearing can act as an effective tool in ice-breaking sessions. Executives in sales and marketing will be taken more seriously by their salespersons in rural hinterland if they can swear appropriately.

While few are aware of potential usages of gaalis, even fewer can apply them because (1) swearing has to happen in vernaculars, and

(2) swearing has to be appropriate. The spirit of swearing is best transmitted in the tongue the receiver speaks in. Dick and *sunni* (Tamil swearword) mean the same thing literally, but *Sunni* is not Dick. The non-technical meanings of these swearwords are different; so also is the impact on person whose mother tongue is Tamil. In order to fully utilise swearing as a weapon you *need to* know vernacular swearing. As a matter of fact, if you don't have the time to learn a new language usage of its swearwords is a crude substitute to become an insider.

Secondly, you need to know the appropriate context and appropriate people with whom swearing works. Else you may end up with a black eye! Also, it must be admitted that swearing does not work in every linguistic region to pop up humour or to break the ice. When it works, severe swears (for instance, incest) may still be offensive. This chapter is a rough guide into the world of on-the-field swearing in various regions of India; 'rough' because I understand if I go wrong and you follow me to the word there are chances that you may land up with a swollen cheek. Swearing is more arts than science and you got to sense the field situation before applying this guide.

South India

There is a marked difference between Dravidian languages and Hindi-derived languages in the sense that incest swearwords are rarely used in the South. The farthest you go with a mother-class cuss is son-of-a-bitch. In Telugu *Lanjha Kodaka* meaning son of a prostitute is a severe curse. *Munda Kodaka* which means son of a widow is more frequently spoken and is less severe.

Tamil happens to be the oldest of all Dravidian languages and perhaps is also the oldest spoken language of the country. This is a language with multinational population base. Inscriptions in Tamil language dating back to 2nd and 1st Century BC have been found in distant places like Egypt and Thailand. Present day you find significant Tamil speaking population in Sri Lanka, Malaysia, Singapore, and in the Caribbean. Tamil is a national language of Singapore; Sri Lanka plunged into a bloody civil war all because Tamil was not accorded national language status!

Hence it is a rewarding proposition to know not just Tamil swearwords but slang words in general. However, colloquial Tamil is vastly different from formal Tamil (also called Centamil). Not just this, there are myriad local dialects which makes it incorrect for us to tag any dialect as 'colloquial Tamil'. Tamil is a diglossic language, i.e. various localised dialects are formed by phonological variations in Centamil. Chennai, Madurai, Coimbatore, Thanjavur all have different spoken Tamil. Dialects in Sri Lanka and in South-East Asia are further different. For example, the gaali for cunt in Chennai Tamil is *pundai* whereas in Kuala Lumpur Tamil it is *Pundah*. The gaali for dick in Chennai Tamil is *sunni*. While *sunni* is part of gaali vocabulary of Kuala Lumpur Tamil, *kambu* is a much more frequently used word for dick there. An exploration of swearwords in these various dialects would be an important contribution to research literature on the subject.

Kena-pundai and *panni* are common swearwords you can use in informal conversation with a Tamil-tongued common man. *Panni* means pig while *kena-pundai* means an idiot. Mark the similarity of this swearword with *chutiya* – both are derived from equivalents of cunt (*chut* and *pundai*) and both mean idiot.

TELUGU cuss basics	
Denga, dengoddu	Fuck
Pooku	Cunt
Puddi, Baayilu	Boobs
Kottukovadam	Masturbate
Madda, modda	Dick
Nee ammani dengoodu	Fuck your mom
Lanjha	Whore
Munda kodaka	Son of a widow

Tamil cuss basics	
Pundai	Cunt
Kottai	Balls
Suni	Dick
Ootha	Fuck
Key-adithal	Masturbate
Thaai-oli	Motherfucker
Okkala-oli	Sister fucker
Muttal	Idiot

Moving up from Tamil Nadu, Karnataka is a state where you will find many swearwords meaning idiot: *tagadu, dabba, pekra* to name a few. Few Kanglish (Kannada + English) gaalis like *cracku* and *mentla* also have the same literal meaning. You can freely use these swearwords when in company of Kannada-speaking pals. With close friends you can also use the words *baddi-magane* (rascal) and *sule-magane* (son of a prostitute).

MALAYALAM cuss basics	
Thullu	Pussy
Thunne	Dick
Keya	Fuck
Thika	Arse
Jyogya	Eunuch
Hadargitti	Bastard

North India

We start the journey of swear survey of North India with Punjab. This is where you find royal patronage to swearing. *Punjab-da-puttar*s love to swear. In this region of the country you may swear on the road to Ludhiana, inside a bar in Patiala, on a busy marketplace, or at the airport in Amritsar; you will find indifference in the expression of those who listen. Swearing is that common here. And no one will make a value judgment about you just because you are foul-mouthed. Punjabi gaalis are harmless, colourful and humorous. What more, they are spoken world over. The high rate of Punjabi migration to places like Canada and UK has effected a cultural diffusion of sorts, and in many towns of UK you will find both Whites and Blacks swearing *teri madi fuddi* (your mother's cunt).

Cross Chandigarh and you reach Haryana, the swear capital of India. There are places in Haryana where people cannot just speak without using a swearword in every sentence. Swearing is like punctuation here. Hindi is spoken fast in Haryanvi dialect and no special change of tone is necessary when emitting a cuss word. The dialect in West UP is also close to Haryanvi; hence you find lot of similarity in swearwords and swearing style of Haryana and West UP. You also find a significant influence of Haryanvi and Punjabi way of swearing in Delhi – after all, the city has a high population of Punjabi and Haryanvi residents.

Up North in the Himalayas various languages are spoken. Dogri in its various dialects is the most widespread languages in the misty Shivaliks and Jammu valley. As is common in most of North India, the most used swearword in Dogri tongue is motherfucker: *maa-iyevia*. When uttering this cuss you have to stretch the 'iyeviaaa' in your speech. A local accent helps in perfecting this swearword. Similarly sister fucker means *pan-iyevia*. The Hindi word *saala* becomes *salyea* in Dogri and the Punjabi *teri madi fuddi* becomes *teri madi seri* (your mother's cunt).

Coming down to the Hindi heartland you will find it hard to make reasonable generalisations. People are quite conscious of *tehzeeb* (manners) in East UP. In the cities of Varanasi and Allahabad I have seen contradictions of sort. People belonging to the society severely censor swearing. But by the banks of Ganges, in these very cities, some of the best poems in foul language are composed. If you mix around with *chillum*-smoking babas, ascetics of the Naga cult or even a *paanwalla* in the area you will get to hear some of the best foul compositions in Hindi. You may even find a hippie (they flock here on the pretext of learning classical music) stoned on a heavy dose of chillum singing gibberish songs in his mother tongue with *maderchod* and *behenchod* prominently featuring in them.

I am told that in a region extending from Far-east UP and West Bihar extending up to river Kosi people speak *theth*. Theth is technically not a language: it simply means foul language. The local dialect of this region is a mixture of Maithili, Bhojpuri, and Hindi. The dialect is nicked *theth* just because people in this region use lots of swearwords. By the way, in Bihar *behenchod* is pronounced *bainchodo*. Both *betichod* and *bainchodo* are popular swearwords in Bihar. *Mooh marao* (literally give a blowjob) is another commonly used swearword. This also applies for Jharkhand, where you find significant Bihari influence. Although Santhali happens to be the state language of Jharkhand, people generally speak Hindi. In interior Jharkhand, however, people still speak Santhali. A common and mild swearword in Santhali is *bhuli inga*, roughly a bitch.

Moving further down the Hindi belt, in Bhopal people have a peculiar swearword delivery style. They shorten cusses. For example, *bhen ka lowda* becomes *bhenkada* and *maa ka lowda* is spoken as *maakda*. Within the Hindi belt *Betichod* is most frequently spoken in Madhya Pradesh. I had read in a blog that the origin of *betichod* is 'basically from Jabalpur in MP' although the blogger did not explain how he reached at this conclusion. Also it is difficult to believe that the origin of so common a cuss can be pinned to a city.

Vidarbha region of Maharashtra has more cultural similarity to MP than Maharashtra. Hence you get to hear *bhenkada* and *maakda* here too. From what I have come to know, the hardcore Marathi belt prefers euphemisms and soft insults over explicit swearwords. For example, *tuzi aai takli* means your mother is bald. *Aai-zhaveda*, the Marathi word for motherfucker, is considered severe in West Maharashtra. However, *aai-zhaveda* is quite common in Mumbai. Often the word is said in humour even if the speaker speaks in Hindi.

A safe gaali you can use with Maharashtrians is *yadzhavya* which means mad fucker.

MARATHI cuss basics	
Zaunya	Fucker
Bullya	Dick
lavadya	Dick
Tuzya aaila puchchi	Your mother's cunt
Tuzya aaila zavala	Fuck your mother
Aaizhaveda	Motherfucker

North-East

Of all the generalisations I make in this chapter, I fear I err most in my treatment of Northeast India. What we club together as 'northeast' is actually a congregation of thousands of cultures and traditions. Linguistically also, languages vary widely. All sixteen Naga tribes of Nagaland, for instance, have their own dialect. In order for them to interact, a language called Nagamese (similar to Assamese) has been made the state language.

Nepali is a widely used language in much of Northeast. Darjeeling in West Bengal, where the movement for Gorkha state is in full sway, is mostly populated by Gorkhas and Lepchas of Nepali origin. Nepali is also a major spoken language in Sikkim, and Nepali gaalis are quite popular there. The language being similar to Hindi, it will be easy for a Hindi speaking person to pick gaalis. Motherfucker is *ma-chik-nay* while *tero ama ko puti* means your mother's dick and *randi ko chorro* means son of a whore.

However, you don't have to use these severe gaalis with anyone unless you are very close to the person. There are other mild and colourful gaalis like *mero lado choos* (suck my dick; Hindi *lawda/ land* becomes *lado* in Nepali), *mero goo kha* (eat my shit) and *kukur chikuwaa* (dog fucker) which can be used to bring in humour when conversing with locals. Remember that swear-dialogue delivery in Nepali has to be fast and shrill.

Nepali cuss basics	
Chikuwaa	Fucker
Lado	Dick
Puti, Muji	Pussy
Geda	Balls
Dudu	Breasts
Jhiyaau	Pubic hair (*jhaant* in Hindi)
Hogg (verb) , goo (noun)	Shit
Kukurni	Bitch

Assamese is one of the few derivatives of Sanskrit which have just a handful of swearwords. In Assam, the most widely used gaali is *kela* which means dick. Another frequently used swearword is *baal-kela which means* pubic hair (literally *baal* – hair - of *kela*). *Kela* in Hindi is banana (which some compare to dick but still is a fruit). So if you are in Assam, don't use the word *kela* when talking to a fruit vendor; the Assamese word for banana is *koola*.

The word for fucker is *soda. Soda* is actually a pollution of the word *choda*, which is derived from the hindi root *chod* (fuck) and means fucker in sister language Bengali. Since 'cha' (?) is non-existent in Assamese dialect, *choda* becomes *soda* in Assamese. Many people in Assam take serious offense to the use of incest gaalis or female genitalia. An acceptable gaali with reference to a relative is *akula-soda*. This is a gaali given to girls and women and means 'your brother is a fucker'.

In the states of Manipur and Mizoram it is better just not to use swearwords. In these states, I have been told, swearing is the tipping point of a physical fight. My friends from these places are just not comfortable uttering any swearword. They tell me that if, say, Aleng swears at Hauthang then Hauthang *has* to fight Aleng as it is a matter of honour. Hauthang has just no option to chicken out. It seems swearing is used in these linguistic areas as a sign daring someone for a duel. In case you ever want to dare a Mizo for a duel, remember that in Mizo *chhu* is pussy and *zang* means dick.

The case of Arunachal Pradesh is an intriguing one. Spoken languages change every few kilometres which makes governance really tough. In the absence of a commonly acceptable language, Hindi has been made the state language. The common man also enthusiastically adopts Hindi and boasts of his Hindi speaking skills. This is because there is a general paranoia among the masses about their land being taken seize by China. China has, for years, claimed that the Monpas (who populate Tawang, West Kameng and East Kameng districts) are culturally more similar to Tibetans than Indians. Hindi helps the people assert their Indian identity.

However, Hindi has the same status here as English has in rest of India: that of a second language. Hence, *chod* is as fashionably spoken in Arunachal towns as fuck is in mainland towns and cities. Owing to their accent, *lowda* may sound like *loura* but essentially gaalis remain the same. *Maderchod* is quite popular, the usage probably adopted from local traders and construction workers who are mostly Biharis and Marwaris.

West Bengal is the far West frontier of North East India. It is said that Bengali is a sweet language. It is referred by some as 'Italian of India'. But then there are Italian swearwords too. Gaalis do not discriminate when populating the tongue of a speaker. The most popular Bengali swearword is *Boka Choda.* This cuss is so frequently used in West Bengal that it has become a mild cuss. Even when the cuss is so generic there is confusion over what the literal meaning of this swear is. I could infer three prominent meanings from my interviews:

1. The receiver is a foolish fucker, i.e. one who cannot fuck properly
2. The receiver fucks a fool
3. The receiver is the offspring of a fool fucking a fool

Most Bengali interviewees subscribed to the first meaning while quite a few were sure that the third meaning is the real semantic basis of the swearword. The first literal interpretation may refer to impotence. The third interpretation is straightaway a reference to parents. Few subscribed to the second meaning; however it appears to me more like a complement. Even if you fuck a fool, you still get to fuck. One interviewee pointed out that this may mean that the receiver's wife/lover is a *boka* (fool).

Shwor (pig) and *kutur* (dog) are other mild swearwords you can use when conversing with a Bengali. *Khanki* and *maggi*, both meaning whore, are words used by women when conversing with women. However these swearwords are considered severe when a man uses them for a woman.

Bengali cuss basics	
Chood	Fuck, fucker
Boga	Dick
Gud	Pussy
Pod	Arse
Khanki, magi	Whore
Kuthi	Bitch
	Khankir pola,
Khankir chhele	Son of a whore
Choodmarani	Motherfucker
Baing chood	Sister fucker

Given the shape and size of this country, this chapter falls terribly short even as a basic guide (may be it will suffice as a dummy's introductory guide). Besides, as you may have realised by now, this write-up lacks extensive research. I ain't no researcher baby. I just like to write nonsense, and hence this. But yeah, I agree with you that a book with extensive research on swearwords in various Indian languages is long due.

APPENDIX

A collection of popular street verses in foul language

Ugly, distasteful, and sexist: verses composed in foul language almost never rise above these three descriptions. Yet they need to be appreciated for being contributions by the common man – idle men of the street - to a vast body of street literature without recognition. This appendix displays a very selective collection of same.

Verse	Remarks
"Door seher mein ek basti thi Wahan ki randi badi sasti thi Gaand mein unki badi masti thi Haat lagao to hasti thi" *After a brief pause when the listener laughs* >tu kyun hasa be?	There was a residential area in a far off city Whores in there were very cheap They had lot of urge in their arse And would shout in joy if you finger them *After a brief pause when the listener laughs, say* >Now why did you laugh?
Ye waqt nahi hai rone ka Ye waqt hai baccha hone ka	This is not the time to cry This is the time to deliver the baby

Abhi kyun royi? Tab to chipak chipak ke soyi Ab kiya hai to bharo Tab kehti thi aur karo	Why do you cry now? Then you used to sleep tightly clinging to your lover Now that you have done it, suffer Then you used to say give me more!
Ehsaan faramosh Maare the hum jo muth[î] Nikle jo muth Aur gira gattar mein To paida huye tum”	Ungrateful you! It was when I had masturbated And when semen had ejaculated And fell in a dirty gutter That you were born
Patthar kya marte ho, pahad maar do Hum tumpe marte hain hamari gaand maar do	Why throw stones at me, throw a hill I love you, won’t mind if you fornicate me in the ass
Cigarette pila pila ke mera jigar jala diya Mangi thi chut to chuttar hila diya	She burnt my heart by making me smoke had asked you your cunt, you blasted I my arse![¥]
Wo aaye hamari kabar par moot ke chale gaye Moot to ek bahana tha choot dikha kar chale gaye	She came to my tomb, pissed, and went away To pee was just an excuse, she actually showed her cunt and went away
Ehsaan kisika liya nahin, mutthi pe gujara karte hain Jab raat ke baara bajte hain hum sadka maara karte hain	Never took a favour [from any girl], I satiate myself with my hands When it strikes twelve in the night I masturbate
Chandni raat mein ek ablah naari apne ghar se nikli Jab land prachand ki dhrishti padi ghanghor ghata mein chapla chamki Jab land se chut hua miland,	A helpless girl came out of her home on a full moon night When our beloved Dick saw the girl there was lightening in the sky And when his dick came together

to chut ki ho gayi puranmasi	with her pussy, pussy was delighted.
Chut chode chutiya, burr chode saitan Beech sadak pe sadka maro, khus rahe bhagwan	Only an idiot fucks a *chut*, only the devil fucks a *burr* [Best thing is] keep masturbating, and God will be happy with you
Ramaiya wata waiya, Ramaiya wata waiya Tune mera mooh mein liya, tune mera mooh mein liya Jamuna pool ke taleee, maine tere mamme male Tune mera chooos liya, tune mera choos liya Tub hi chudi, teri maa bhi chudi Teri naani ne chudne ka waada kiya	*This is a modification of a popular Hindi movie song. This song has to be sung in the same tune as the original, just the lyrics has been modified to include swearwords.*
BOY: Matak matak ke chalti ho kya maar hi dalogi Thoda sa hame bhi do kya achaar dalogi GIRL: Matak matak ke chalti hun meri chaal hi aisi hai Ghar jake dekho sabki ek hi jaisi hai	BOY: The way you do that catwalk, seems I will die [of desire] Let me taste [some of you], what else will you do: add preservatives [to keep the beauty from being wasted]? GIRL:I do a catwalk, that's how I walk Go home and see [your mom's and sister's], all [women] walk the same way
BOY: Sau kamata hun sawa sau lutata hun, tumhare jaisi randion ko apne laude pe bithata hun GIRL: Sau kamate ho sawa sau lutate ho. Pachis rupaiya kya gaand marake late ho? Gand phate to phate Power kabhi na ghate	BOY: I earn a hundred, spend hundred and twenty five; I consider whores like you no better than my dick GIRL: You earn a hundred, spend hundred and twenty five; Do you get the extra twenty five as fees for getting sodomised? *Essence of this saying is whatever be the difficulties in life, you should not lose hope*

Dhanno chud gayi, Bano chud gayi, chud gaye parmanand Sath saal ki budhia chud gayi, bahu ke nikle land	Dhanno got fucked, Bano got fucked, even the Lord got fucked The old woman of sixty got fucked, when the daughter-in-law got a dick[n]
Galib chadhe pahad pe Deen land latkaye Jako jitna chahiye kaat kaat le jaye	
6 commandments to be followed all through life: 1. Chut, chuchi aur chillum jitni bhi piyo kabhi jhooti nahi hoti 2. Bhajan, Bhojan aur chodan hamesha ekant mein hi karna chahiye 3. Phoda, lauda, aur ghoda sahlane se badhta hai 4. Lund aur ghamand dono ko kabu mein rakhna chahiye 5. Saamp aur chut jahan dekho maar do 6. Hanuman chalisa aur condom hamesha paas rakho. Bhoot aur chut ka pata nahi kab mil jaye	6 commandments to be followed all through life: 1. Cunt, nipples and *chillum* are never polluted by taste 2. One should always do prayer, fooding and sex in privacy 3. Bodily boils, penis, and horses evolve when they are scratched 4. One should keep his dick and pride in control 5. Wherever you see a snake or cunt, *maar do* (can mean kill it or fuck it) 6. Always carry Hanuman Chalisa and condom with you. You are never sure when you would find a ghost or a cunt
Chut chut sab ek hi Ek hi chut ka rang Kali ho ya gori Chodo prem ke sang Chodo prem ke sang Chut ki mahima aisi Land jaye murjhaye Chut waisi ki waisi	All cunt are the same Same is the colour of cunt Black or white Fuck with love and adulation Fuck with love and adulation Such is the miracle of cunts Dick may grow old [and not go erect] But cunt remains the same

Land bada prachand Land pe badal chayo Land hi dulha, Land hi dulhann, Land barati aayo Daal mein land, bhaat mein land, land hi bhog lagayo Teri maa ki chut mein behen ke land tu humko land dikhayo?	*An irrelevant song on land (*dick*) comparing dick to everything that is important: fame, marriage, food, offering to God.*
GUY: Kash mein teri kacchi hota Tujhse nahi to teri chut se chipka hota GIRL: Kash tu mera kacchi hota Mein ek jagaha chud rahi hoti tu doosre jagaha pada rehta	GUY: I wish I was your panty If not you, I would have got to cling to your cunt GIRL: I wish you were my panty I would be getting fucked at one place, you would be lying at another place
Jokhun amar lichu lichu Sabai amar pichu pichu Jakhun amar aam aam Tokhun amar daam daam Jokhun amar dab dab Tokhun amar bhab bhab Jokhun amar jhule gelo Sabae amake bhule gelo	When my [boobs] were the size of lichi fruit Everyone was running after me When my [boobs] were like mango fruit Then there was high demand for me When my [boobs] were the size of coconut Then I was pampered But when my [boobs] slackened and hung loose Everyone forgot me

Notes

1 Karjalainen (2002), p.4.

2 Andersson and Trudgill (1990), p.53.

3 Wordweb dictionary definition

4 Jay (2000), p.85.

5 *Sadakchap* literally means 'derived from the streets'. Sadakchap language refers to slang dialects used in streets and bazaars. These slang dialects are proletarian in nature and are looked down upon by the elite. Hence the word sadakchap is used with a negative connotation.

6 Definition retrieved from http://en.wikipedia.org/wiki/Sexual_objectification

7 See, for example, Swain (2009), p.225; Benokraitis (1997).

8 Tanning and selling leather is the traditional occupation of *chamar* caste community.

9 *Jana* means tribe and *Jati* means caste society, and this divide has been in our society to differentiate so called civilized people living in close proximity with tribals.

10 Extracted from http://paritosh-chakma.blogspot.com/2009/06/say-no-to-discrimination-in-india-too.html on 20th April, 2010.

11 Personal interview; also see http://www.blogbharti.com/kuffir/caste/us-and-vais-in-the-north-east/, as referred to on 20th April, 2010.

12 See, for example, Bhat, A. 'New Levels of Terrorism, Corruption in Manipur' in Asian Age. Extracted from http://www.asianage.com/index.php?option=com_content&view=article&id=9593:new-levels-of-terrorism-corruption-in-manipur&catid=51:news-plus&Itemid=79 on 29th April, 2010.

13 *Kafir* should not be confused with *kaffir or kaffer* which is an offensive word for a black person in South Africa.

14 Scheduled Caste (SC) is a legal term referring to the depressed sections of society who now collectively call themselves Dalit. Scheduled Tribe (ST) is the legal term for tribal communities.

15 Data collected from personal interviews; data on Sri Lanka from http://www.statemaster.com/encyclopedia/Sri-Lankan-Tamil-slang-and-swear-words.

16 Data collected from personal interviews; data on Sri Lanka from http://www.statemaster.com/encyclopedia/Sri-Lankan-Tamil-slang-and-swear-words.

17 For a detailed outline of etymology and interpretation of *Mleccha* over the ages, see Parasher (1991).

18 Advertising Standard Authority Website http://www.asa.org.uk/NR/rdonlyres/1EAEACA7-8322-4C86-AAC2-4261551F57FE/0/ASA_Delete_Expletives_Dec_2000.pdf, retrieved on 15.3.2006.

19 Extracted from news item http://www.nytimes.com/2005/05/02/opinion/02herbert.html?_r=1 on 24th April, 2010.

20 Retrieved from www.urbandictionary.com on 24th April, 2010.

21 Wikipedia.

22 Compiled based on data from personal interviews and the following sources: http://www.rsdb.org/, Wikipedia, http://www.bookrags.com/wiki/List_of_ethnic_slurs.

23 Jay (2009).

24 See http://en.wikipedia.org/wiki/Blasphemy

25 Garg (2000).

26 *Ibid.*

27 Note that this is not based on any systematic study, nor is the frequency of use of these swearwords in the same order as mentioned here.

28 See Kakar (1978).

29 Pradhan (2008).

30 Kakar (1978).

31 Kandiyoti (1997), p.89-90.

32 Later when this child would grow up and marry, a new *bahu* will enter this family. Then this woman (the mother) becomes a *saas* and will try her best to marginalise the *bahu*, thereby starting another *saas-bahu* political warfare in the household. Every woman goes through a *nanad-bahu-saas* cycle in traditional patriarchy (Swain, 2009b). Hence the appeal of *saas-bahu* serials among Indian women.

33 Allen (1982).

34 Pradhan (2008)

35 While *mitakshara* system of inheritance is followed in rest of the patriarchal belt, *dayabhaga* system is followed in Bengal. *Dayabhaga* system allows women to inherit property that belonged to the Hindu undivided family.

36 This is not based on any empirical fact, but on folk belief.

37 See Gupta (2000).

38 See Dundes (1997), p.92-93.

39 Now India is too big a country to make generalizations regarding toilet training, but this is the general trend.

40 Wajnryb (2005), p.15.

41 Pappu is an euphemism for dick.

42 See Vanita & Kidwai (2001), p.27-28.

43 Kakar (1982), p. 134-135, quoted in Cohen (2000), p. 164-165. Italics mine.

44 Cohen (2008), p. 165.

45 MN Srinivas had introduced the concept of 'dominant caste' to explain why local caste hierarchy can be different from universal caste hierarchy determined as per ritual purity – ritual pollution. Local hierarchy is determined by numerical strength and economic well being. Hence, in a local hierarchy castes of Brahmin and Kshatriya *varna* may be placed lower than castes of Vaishya or Sudra *varna*.

46 For a concise dealing of Indian research on individualism-collectivism, see Verma, J. (2004).

47 Pinker (2007).

48 See Montagu (1967, p.77-78), Karjalainen (2002, p.26-27).

49 Jay (2009).

50 Chootiyum Sulphate is a derivative of Chutiya and Sodium Sulphate. Though the exact origin of this expression is not clear, evidently it's a lingo first used by college students with chemistry as a subject. This lingo has been in use in Allahabad University for quite some time now, although the real source is probably a smaller college from the hinterland.

51 See Jay (2009).

52 Swain (2009), p.229.

53 In some Tamil dialects of Sri Lanka, the word *saniyan* is used by mothers to scold their children. This swear is also derived from a God's name; *Sani* (Saturn) is a notorious God feared for the bad fortune He brings to people.

54 See Dooling (1996, p.8), for example. In fact, Dooling has forwarded a biological explanation to the gender difference. He reasons that (p.10) studies have confirmed that cerebral cortex located higher up in brain is the neural source of normal language. However, swearing is controlled by more primitive subcortical structures in the brain stem. Yet other studies confirm that men use these

subcortical structures more often than women, hence providing an evidence for biological causation of gender differences in swearing.

55 Garg (2000).

56 Quoted from an article by Dan Majestic: "Of Swearing: Use the F-word properly: Otherwise it loses its sparkle" retrieved from http://www.stirringtroubleinternationally.com/2010/07/12/of-swearing-use-the-f-word-properly-otherwise-it-loses-its-sparkle/ on 13th June, 2010.

57 Jones (2007).

58 Mellem (2007).

59 Ibid.

60 The Islamic purdah, argue rightwing Hindu ideologues, was adopted into Hinduism which devalued women's status in Hindu society too. However, historical research has proved that Hindu women covered their faces even before establishment of Islamic rule.

61 Some of these are education and social mobility, resistance from newly ascendant castes, land reforms, and progressive laws.

62 K. A. Abbas Vs. Union of India (1970 (2) SCC 780).

63 Bobby Art International v. Om Pal Singh Hoon and Others (**1996 (4) SCC 1**).

64 Ibid

65 Stephens, Atkins & Kingston (2009).

66 Ross (1960).

References

Allen, Michael (1982) 'Introduction: The Hindu View of Women' in Allen, Michael and Mukherjee, SN (Eds) 'Women in India and Nepal'. Canberra: Australian National University

Andersson, L.-G. & Trudgill, Peter (1990) Bad Language. Blackwell: Oxford.

Benokraitis, N.V. (1997) Subtle sexism: Current practice and prospects for change. Sage: CA

Cohen, Lawrence (2008) No Aging in India: Alzheimer's, The Bad Family, and Other Modern Things. University of California Press: California

Dundes, Alan (1997) Two tales of crow and sparrow: a Freudian folkloristic essay on caste and untouchability. Rowman & Littlefield: Maryland

Garg, Mridula (2000) Word as Censor. *Economic and Political Weekly*, Vol. 35, No. 18 (Apr. 29 - May 5, 2000), pp. WS7-WS9

Gupta, Dipankar (2000) Interrogating Caste: Understanding Hierarchy and Difference in Indian Society. Penguin Books: New Delhi

Hughes, Geoffrey (2006) An Encyclopedia of swearing: The social history of oaths, profanity, foul language, and ethnic slurs in the English speaking world.

Jay, T. (2009) The Utility and Ubiquity of Taboo Words. Retrieved on 3rd April, 2010 from http://www.mcla.edu/Undergraduate/uploads/textWidget/1457.00016/documents/Jay_Taboo.pdf

Jay, T. (2000) Why we curse. John Benjamins: Philadelphia

Jones (2007) Offensive language: I Think My Mother Taught Me. Retrieved from http://tallskinnykiwi.typepad.com/tallskinnykiwi/2007/06/offensive_langu.html on

April 10th, 2010.

Kakar, Sudhir (1978) The Inner World: A Psycho-Analytic Study of Childhood and Society in India

Kandiyoti, Deniz (1997) 'Bargaining with Patriarchy' in Viswanathan, Nalini and Duggan, Lynn and Nisonoff, Laurie and Wiegersma, Nan (Eds) 'The Woman, Gender and Development Reader'. Zubaan: New Delhi

Karjalainen, Markus (2002) Where have all the swearwords gone? An analysis of the loss of swearwords in two Swedish translations of J. D. Salinger's Catcher in the Rye. Post Graduation thesis, Department of English, University of Helsinki. Retrieved on 5th February, 2010 from http://ethesis.helsinki.fi/julkaisut/hum/engla/pg/karjalainen/wherehav.pdf.

Mellem, Adam (2007) A Theology of Profanity. Retrieved from http://tallskinnykiwi.typepad.com/tallskinnykiwi/files/a_theology_of_profanity.pdf on 9th April, 2010.

Montagu, Ashley (1967) The Anatomy of Swearing. Macmillan: New York

Parasher, A. (1991)Mlecchas in Early India. Munishiram Manoharlal: N. Delhi

Pinker, Steven (2007) The stuff of thought: Language as a window to human nature. Viking: New York

Pradhan, Anubhav (2008) Teri Maa ki: An analysis of common swear words. Retrieved from http://ap-city-of-dijns.blogspot.com/2008/10/teri-ma-ki-analysis-of-common-swear.html on 9th April, 2010.

Ross, Helen (1960) Patterns of swearing. Discovery. Nov 1960, 479-481.

Stephens, R. Atkins, J. & Kingston, A. (2009) Swearing as a response to pain. Neuroreport. 2009 Aug 5;20(12):1056-60.

Swain, Smarak (2009) Applied Psychology: Cross-cultural and India-centric Perspectives. New Vishal Publications: New Delhi.

Vanita, Ruth & Kidwai, Saleem (2001). Same-sex love in India: readings from literature and history. Palgrave Macmillan

Wajnryb, Ruth (2005) Expletive Deleted: A Good Look at Bad Language. Free Press.

ACKNOWLEDGEMENTS

This book is the product of one pair of hands and many brains. My sincere thanks to my friends Vaibhav Jain, Sridhar Dora, Prashant Babu Kodali, Priyadarshi Mishra, Amit Anand, Rituraj Mishra, Nilabhra Dasgupta, Vijay Tadia, Anbu Selvam, Rajiv Ranjan Singh, Binit Mund, Ashutosh Mohapatra, Basavraj Hiremath and Vipul Waghmare and a host of others who are not comfortable having their name in this book ☺. I am grateful to Niharika Singh, Abi Rama Karthikeyan, Sandeep Lakra, S. Sundar Rajan, Jeevan Tudu, Priya Malshe and Anjai Lal for going through various draft copies and giving fruitful feedback.

I am indebted to graphics designer Rahul Dora for designing the cover page. Also to RSK Reddy and Dibyabandana Nayak at Learnitude Academy for helping me give the book a finishing touch.

My gratitude to luck for getting me in touch with Jayantada of Srishti publications, a publisher who soon became a pal; an editor who made all out efforts to get this book published in its present format in a short time.

Lastly, my gratitude to numerous lady friends – both personal and via social network – who went through various drafts of chapter 3 and gave their feedback. In that chapter my intention was to demonstrate the use of sexist galis among she allow make youth (which can be pretty pinching and ugly) and then denounce them. The challenge was to demonstrate the severity of such gaalis without offending an entire gender. Many drafts were prepared for that chapter till a balance could be reached at and I thank all those lady friends who contributed to censoring and editing of that chapter.

I heavily depended on Wikipedia as a source for interesting facts and ideas. It's a great website to mine from. This not being a non-fiction by definition I have not cared to make a meticulous reference note. However, I have detailed various sources I have referred to in bibliography.

SPANDAN BISWAL

B.A.LLB (Hons.) | Advocate | Orissa State Bar Council | Enrolment No. 0 – 1044/29

Privileged and Confidential

To
Mr. Smarak Swain,
E-10, Shyamali Colony
Doranda, Ranchi-2

Dear Sir,

I have perused the draft of your book titled "Beep You! You Beephole: The Black book of Indian Cuss and Slurs" sent by on January 22, 2011 by email.

Query:

Section 292 (1) of the Indian Penal Code, 1860 provides that:

"For the purposes of sub-section (2), a book, pamphlet, paper, writing, drawing, painting, representation, figure or any other object, shall be deemed to be obscene if it is lascivious or appeals to the prurient interest or if its effect, or (where it comprises two or more distinct items) the effect of any one of its items, is, if taken as a whole, such as to tend to deprave and corrupt persons who are likely, having regard to all relevant circumstances, to read, see or hear the matter contained or embodied in it.]

.....

Exception-This section does not extend to-

(a) Any book, pamphlet, paper, writing, drawing, painting, representation or figure-

(i) The publication of which is proved to be justified as being for the public good on the ground that such book, pamphlet, paper, writing, drawing, painting, representation or figure is in the interest of science, literature, art of learning or other objects of general concern, or

(ii) Which is kept or used bona fide for religious purposes."

In this context you require us to provide our legal opinion regarding the applicability of the said section to the draft book.

Analysis:

SPANDAN BISWAL

B.A.LLB (Hons.) | Advocate | Orissa State Bar Council | Enrolment No. O – 1044/29

Privileged and Confidential

The broad principles of interpretation of the said section have been laid down by the Supreme Court in *Ranjit D. Udeshi* v. *State Of Maharashtra*[1] wherein the court has said:

1) "It may, however, be said at once that treating with sex and nudity in art and literature cannot be regarded as evidence of obscenity without something more.";
2) "The Court must, therefore, apply itself to consider each work at a time. This should not, of course, be done in the spirit of the lady who charged Dr. Johnson with putting improper words in his Dictionary and was rebuked by him - "Madam, you must have been looking- for them." To adopt such an attitude towards art and literature would make the courts a board of censors.";
3) "An overall view of the obscene matter in the setting of the whole work would, of course, be necessary, but the obscene matter must be considered by itself and separately to find out whether it is so gross and its obscenity so decided that it is likely to deprave and corrupt those whose minds are open to influences of this sort and into whose hands the book is likely to fall.";

And crucially,

4) **"the test to adopt in our country (regard being had to our community mores) is that obscenity without a preponderating social purpose or profit cannot have the constitutional protection of free speech and expression, and obscenity is treating with sex in a manner appealing to the carnal side of human nature, or having that tendency."**

The said book contains a study of words of abuse presently in use in Indian society. Such words are in common usage and hence cannot be held to be violative of public decency as that such interpretation would mean that an entire generation of people commit a crime everyday.

The abusive words, if interpreted in a literal sense deal with sexual organs or sexual connotations, or nonsense; but if interpreted in the context in which they are normally used in the modern Indian languages, do not deal with sex, nor can they be interpreted as appealing to the carnal side. Further, the said book does not use them as a pornographic material, designed to titilate; it is a compendium of the present contexts and usages of those words and phrases.

Most importantly the said book is in the nature of a linguistic study, whose very purpose is to elaborate the ideas expressed in the paragraph above. Given these reasons, it is not possible to construe that the said book appeals to the prurient interest.

Hence it is my opinion that the said section does not apply to this draft book.

Regards,

Spandan Biswal

7/2/11

[1] 1965 AIR 881